Too Much Is
Not Enough

Too Much Is Not Enough

A Memoir of Fumbling Toward Adulthood

Andrew Rannells

CROWN
ARCHETYPE
NEW YORK

All rights reserved.
Published in the United States by Crown Archetype,
an imprint of the Crown Publishing Group, a division of
Penguin Random House LLC, New York.
crownpublishing.com

Crown Archetype and colophon is a registered trademark of
Penguin Random House LLC.

"My Second Date with Brad" first appeared in a slightly different form
in the *New York Times* Modern Love column on July 28, 2017.

Lyrics from "Wicked Little Town" from *Hedwig and the Angry Inch*
provided courtesy of Stephen Trask.

Library of Congress Cataloging-in-Publication Data is available.

ISBN 978-0-525-57485-9
Ebook ISBN 978-0-525-57487-3

Printed in the United States of America

Book design by Lauren Dong
Jacket design by Zak Tebbal
Jacket photograph courtesy of the National YoungArts Foundation

10 9 8 7 6 5 4 3 2 1

First Edition

Baby, I'll be tough
Too much is not enough . . .

—"Fame" by Michael Gore and Dean Pitchford
(and originally belted out by Irene Cara)

Contents

About Andrew Rannells

(The Honest Version)

This is maybe not going to be what you think it's going to be.

When I have to provide a bio for a *Playbill* or a television show announcement or the jacket of the book you're holding in your hand, I'm always struck by how tidy it looks. Each sentence contains an achievement that I'm proud of, something that for years I had only dreamed could be possible. I've worked hard, and I'm happy to say that I have achieved much of what I set out to do when I first moved to New York in 1997. (I mean, I would still like to have a weekly brunch date with Stephen Sondheim, but it's always good to have goals.)

But my biography is also deceiving. It's all highs and no lows, with bullet points of good stuff and none of the details of the in-between, and it starts with me starring in my third Broadway show, when I was thirty-two. In reality, my bio should include sentences like:

Prior to being cast in The Book of Mormon, *Andrew left his family in Omaha, Nebraska, missed them terribly, and often wondered if he had made the right choice to leave his home.*

Or:

After starring in Hairspray *on Broadway as the third Link Larkin, Andrew faced months of unemployment and thought he would never work again. During that time, he loved to stress eat, spiraled into regularly scheduled anxiety attacks, and had to take a job as a temp at Ernst & Young. He still couldn't tell you what he was supposed to be doing at that job, because he mostly hid in either the men's bathroom or the break room.*

Or:

In his free time, Andrew likes to drink wine with friends, watch countless consecutive hours of HGTV, and manage panic about his personal life.

(Just a side note: You know how, at the end of *Our Town*, the Stage Manager lets Emily go back and pick one day in her life to visit? One of my greatest fears is that this will happen to me when I die and I will accidentally pick a day that I spent alone in my apartment eating large Domino's pizzas and watching an entire season of *Mad Men* straight through. Like, all thirteen hours at once. Actually, maybe there's nothing wrong with that day.)

What these official bios always leave out are the years I had in New York City before I was working on Broadway. Before I was in *The Book of Mormon* and *Girls*. Before people started stopping me on the subway to say, "Did we go to high school together?" (Unless you attended an all-boys Jesuit Catholic high school in Omaha, Nebraska, . . . no, we did not.) Or "I love you on *Modern Family*!" (Actually, that's Jesse Tyler Ferguson.) Or my all-time favorite, "Tell me why I know you!" (Ma'am, that's a question only you can answer.)

These missing years were messy and confusing and filled with questionable choices, and for a long time I was happy to omit them. But I realize now just how much happened during that period of my life—a time when I was excited, and terrified, on a daily basis about what the future held for me—

and I wanted to tell some stories about experiences that have been just as important as all of those highlights in my bio.

Everyone who leaves home, with dreams of making it in the city, starts somewhere, and I'm pretty sure that my dream began at a young age, when my dad started showing me MGM and Warner Bros. musicals from the forties and fifties. Judy Garland, Betty Grable, Gene Kelly, Dick Haymes. I idolized all of them. My love of older movie musicals led to a love of newer movie musicals like *Fame, Little Shop of Horrors,* and *Grease 2* (I prefer the sequel to the original; I know I'm not alone here).

Because of this love of musicals, my mom suggested I watch the Tony Awards one year. I was instantly hooked. It was so much better than the movies; it was *live*! I would watch the Tonys every year and dream about being one of those people on the stage performing. It was the 1993 Tony Awards that really sealed the deal. The casts of *Kiss of the Spider Woman, Blood Brothers, The Goodbye Girl,* and *The Who's Tommy* all performed that night, and I fell madly in love with every minute of the telecast. That was the moment I knew that I didn't want to be just a fan, I wanted to be one of them. I wasn't sure how I was going to do it, but I knew I had to figure it out. My family, while incredibly supportive, didn't have the answers, either. I thought I would start with the most obvious first step and just go from there; I had to get myself to New York City.

I see the new kids arriving in the city every year, new faces ready to tackle their dreams, practically shouting, "God, I hope I get it! I hope I get it!" I want to welcome them and tell them what they can expect, what I wish I had known when I first arrived. At the top of that list: It might look like people are ahead of you, be it in money, looks, or opportunity, but here's what—Eyes on your own paper, folks! Everyone has to do the work. People who just get handed opportunity without the effort usually fuck it up and end up much lower than when they started. Your career is something that starts with the first step, not with a promotion or a movie or an award. It begins the minute you say you are going to do it. So make it all count.

I can't give you a shortcut, because there isn't one, so the following pages are not a guide to making it in New York. Instead, they are stories of wins, big and small, of falling down but always getting up, and of experiencing everything you possibly can and making a life to be proud of along the way. That's all a lofty way to say you are about to read about homesickness, bad auditions, good auditions, sex with the wrong person, occasionally sex with the right person (who generally turns out to be the wrong person), some unfortunate but inescapable life events on the path to adulthood, and lots of wine with friends along the way.

If I could squeeze all of these stories into the bio on the jacket of this book, I would. But my editor won't let me, so please consider this book the longer, more honest version of my bio—the one I'd share with a friend over a few drinks. I should also add that some names and personal details have been changed. I tried to be as accurate as possible, but, let's be honest, we all know how memory works. For example, as I was writing many of these stories, I imagined myself as a young Leonardo DiCaprio in them, but after consulting some photo albums, I realized that simply wasn't the case. I hope you enjoy my stories anyway.

Too Much Is Not Enough

My Entrance

IT WAS AUGUST IN NEW YORK, WHICH I DIDN'T YET know is the lousiest month of the year here. The air is thick and damp, and you constantly have the feeling that you're in a steam room fueled entirely by urine. The line for taxis at Newark Airport already seemed beaten down by the heat, and given that I wasn't even in Manhattan yet, I couldn't help but interpret the scene as some kind of warning about how hard the city was going to be. But I was here. I had taken the biggest step and I had moved to New York City. Though I had only visited a couple times in prior years, I knew this was where I belonged. I was falling in love like a kid falls in love at summer camp—quickly, completely, and with irrational passion. After nearly thirty painful minutes, my sweat-drenched parents and I piled into a cab like cattle, adding physical discomfort to the emotional awkwardness that had marked the trip so far.

I should mention here that three days before we'd left Omaha, the week I'd turned nineteen, I'd come out to my family. (I didn't think there would be an issue, but just in case, I had an exit firmly planned.) My family was mostly, what's the best way to say this? Not shocked. I knew all the words to *Grease 2* by the time I was six. I played around the house *as* Miss Piggy. I watched *T.J. Hooker* hoping that Adrian Zmed would be shirtless at some point. He rarely disappointed. And then there was the telltale sign: I was obsessed with *The Wizard of Oz*. Even the black-and-white part. So here we were, my parents and I, three days out of the closet, jammed into the back of a cab that was swerving toward Manhattan, making us all carsick. The anxiety was thicker than the Nag Champa the cabdriver was burning on the dashboard. Neither one of my parents had come with me to look at colleges, and it was clear that they didn't want to be on this trip, either.

My father, Ron, had never set foot in New York, and he didn't seem excited about doing so now. We had never been close, and I already worried that coming out had created more of a distance between us. Now there would be a physical distance, too. I knew there would be no long phone calls sharing the drama of drama school with him, or hearing him tell me about the stresses of his advertising sales business. The chance for a relationship with him as a young adult was looking slimmer and slimmer.

My mother, Charlotte, a former teen model from Omaha, hadn't been to New York since she was a high school student in 1964. She and some other local girls from her modeling agency had been taken to Manhattan to meet talent agents, and while she had been presented with the opportunity of staying in New York, city life had proved too hectic and she had returned to Nebraska. While she always spoke romantically about her visit—the excitement of staying at the Waldorf Astoria, going to the Russian Tea Room, seeing Robert Redford in *Barefoot in the Park*—she had never returned, not until this trip.

No one in my family had gone away to college, and not only was I going away, I was going 1,249 miles away. My coming out, combined with my move, filled my mother with every fear imaginable: muggings, gay bashings, me being sex trafficked. The first time I'd gone to New York to look at schools, she had given me a roll of quarters and told me, "You can use them for vending machines or pay phones or hold them in your fist and punch someone if they try to attack you." Beyond arming me with coins as a means of self-defense, my parents had made it clear that they wouldn't be helping me with college costs or the expense of moving to New York. I can't explain to you why my parents took this stance, but in my family, college was something you paid for yourself. I had watched my two older sisters and my brother do it. They studied hard for scholarships, they worked multiple jobs, and they managed. Now it was my turn. But no one was willing to say, or perhaps no one understood, just how different, and difficult, New York City was going to be.

I had started working at a young age, doing TV commercials and local modeling jobs, and had saved a few thousand dollars over the years—enough to get started, but not nearly enough for college. So when the time came to audition for drama departments, I had no choice but to base my choices on price. I was given a full ride to Marymount Manhattan College—and was grateful for the opportunity—but I knew instantly, somewhere in my heart, that it was not the best fit. Still, while it wasn't the school of my dreams—that was NYU—it was putting me geographically closer to an even bigger dream of acting on Broadway, a dream that suddenly felt real for the first time as the lights of Times Square flashed in front of me. The cab ride through Manhattan had felt almost as long as the plane ride, but finally we pulled up at what would be my new home for this new stage of my life.

The dorm was an old building on 57th and Lexington. It's a neighborhood I know now is soulless and sad, but on that first day, it seemed terribly glamorous. The building was called the Allerton Hotel. In my head it was going to be a normal dorm experience, with common rooms and dry erase boards on the doors and clove cigarettes in the quad. We walked into the lobby and my mother gasped. It wasn't THAT bad, but it was . . . bad. It wasn't so much a dorm as it was a welfare hotel with a handful of floors for Marymount students. If you live in New York or have ever visited, you know those old people you see on the street who are wearing all of their coats in summer and a Duane Reade bag as a hat? Who have a cat on a leash or a dirty dog in a stroller and are yelling to everyone and no one things like "It's coming! I'm telling you it's coming! When it happens you can remember I told you first! You fucking whore!"? Do you know the people I am talking about? They all lived in this building. And I was going to share a bathroom and a shower with some of them. In that moment I was so self-absorbed that I could only see these people as harbingers of my potential future—a *Twilight Zone* mirror of what New York City can do to people. Now I understand that the residents at the Allerton probably weren't too pleased to have a bunch of drama students invading their home, blasting *Chess* at all hours and kick-ball-changing their way down the halls. It was not the best arrangement for anyone.

My parents were also processing our surroundings. I sensed their bodies slowing down the minute we walked into the lobby, like they were turning into stone. Or maybe they thought that if they stayed very still, we could all just pretend we weren't where we were. I, on the other hand, pretended things were going great. I marched up to the Marymount representative, announced myself, and waited for him to welcome me with open arms. He barely made eye contact, muttered "Welcome," and told me I'd be living on the twelfth floor and that the elevator was *very* slow, so we should probably take the stairs. Eleven flights. Two Midwestern parents. August in New York. No air-conditioning. We trudged up those stairs, stopping periodically to breathe and manage our panic. The hallways were narrow and dark, but there were several other cheerful freshmen and their parents running about. It seemed like everyone was having a better time than the Rannells family.

I was determined to turn this around. I started making jokes and talking about how exciting it all was. How much character the building had. My parents weren't playing along. We got to my room, I opened the door, and we all attempted to walk inside. It was probably eight feet by ten feet, with a low twin bed, a tiny sink, a bare bulb hanging from the ceiling, and one window that faced a darkened airshaft. My mother burst into tears.

"God damn it, Charlotte," my father said. "It's not that bad."

"Yeah, Mom, it's going to be fine."

But I knew better. All the *Rebel Without a Cause* movie posters and all the Bath & Body Works linen spray in the mall were not going to save this cell. (Since I had just come out of the closet, I hadn't yet attained the Gay Decorating Wonder Powers that I have now.)

At the time I couldn't suggest we all slam a couple drinks

and then deal with what was in front of us, so I suggested we go eat instead. We walked back down the eleven flights of stairs, my mother trying not to cry, my father not speaking. "One of the best parts about New York is that no matter where you go, there are great restaurants," I said, annoying myself with my own pluck.

As it turns out, there were no restaurants at 57th and Lexington. We walked around a bit, and I started to realize that this neighborhood was not the New York of my dreams. The last time I'd visited, I'd stayed on the Upper West Side and hung out in the West Village—places that looked like the set of *Seinfeld* or *Friends*. (I didn't know at the time that both shows were filmed on studio lots in Los Angeles.) This neighborhood looked like the saddest office party on the planet. Eventually we found a diner that looked acceptable. The waiter shouted at us in a manner that made us all uncomfortable, and food eventually arrived. It wasn't exactly what we ordered, but no one said anything. I worked overtime to assure my parents that this move was exactly what I'd been expecting and that I was excited and thrilled to be in New York. They seemed sad and doubtful, but they managed to smile.

After lunch we walked around a bit more, and then we found our way back to the Allerton. I asked my parents what they wanted to do that night. I imagined showing them how I could already navigate the TKTS booth or how easy it was to use the subway. My father instead said, "We are going to check into our hotel and let you get settled in. We should have breakfast tomorrow, if you have time." My mom just stood there. It was 4:30 p.m. *SETTLED IN?!* I thought. They had seen the room; all I had to do was open my suitcase and I was "settled in." What did they think I was going to do? "I heard one of the other parents talking about orientation, so you'll probably have to do that tonight too," my mother managed to say. "*THAT IS TOMORROW AFTERNOON!*" I wanted to scream. "*I have nothing to do and I hate where I live and I am terrified, please do not leave me!*" But instead I said, "Great. I will meet you at your hotel in the morning." Then I put them in a cab and walked back into my new home, up those eleven flights of stairs, past all the other students and parents unpacking shower caddies and tiny microwave ovens, and into my cell. I shut the door and locked it behind me. And then I cried. I cried like I had never cried in my life. This was my dream, moving to New York and starting my life as an adult, and it was horrible.

I don't know how long I cried, but it was a while. Finally, I stopped. I decided that I couldn't spend my first day in New York feeling sorry for myself. I summoned the Midwestern grit of my ancestors, the strength and spirit of Willa Cather and her prairie kin, and decided I needed to take charge of my experience. Unlike other college dorms, these cells were only meant for one person. Initially the "no roommate" detail had seemed like a plus, but now I realized that I alone was going to have to make this room acceptable. I unpacked my clothes and put them in my tiny closet. I made my bed and sprayed my eucalyptus Bath & Body Works linen spray everywhere. I arranged a few family photos I had packed, and then I sat back and took in my new home. It wasn't bad.

Just as my stress level started to decline, I heard people outside in the halls talking and laughing and yelling about extension cords, flip-flops for the shower, and Beds in a Bag (popular in 1997). I wanted to go out and say hello, but I was too embarrassed—embarrassed that I didn't have any of that fun stuff that's meant to make a dorm room livable, and that I was alone. I couldn't stay in that room any longer. *Fuck it,* I thought. *This is New York City and I'm living here now.* I marched down those stairs for the fourth time that day, looked for a pay phone, and then called the one person who I knew in the city: Celestina Villanueva.

I had met Celestina at a college scholarship audition earlier that year, and we had kept in touch. She had a low, vaguely Southern drawl and a job as a hostess at a wine bar in Dallas, which seemed like the most mature job a person our age could have. As a kid, I loved the TV show *It's a Living,* which followed the lives of the waitresses at a penthouse bar in Los Angeles. I could easily picture Celestina next to Ann Jillian, serving drinks and slinging wisecracks. She fit perfectly in my dream version of life in New York.

I knew that Celestina was already living in the NYU dorms, so I dropped in my coin and called the number she had sent me. Much to my relief, she answered. I tried to sound calm and natural and crossed my fingers for an invitation. After listening to her talk about her "brilliant movement teacher" for two more quarters, she finally said it: "Come see my dorm!" That was it. That's what I needed. She told me to take the R train, which was magically the one I was standing right by, and she said the stop was 8th Street/NYU. How easy was this? I purchased my token, got on my train, stood instead of sat—so as to look more confident—and exited at my stop. I was slightly unclear as to exactly which neighborhood I was in, but it was immediately apparent that *this* was closer to the New York I had imagined. There were young people everywhere, laughing and playing hacky sack, wearing fishnets. And drinking coffee. At night! A man played a plastic bucket as a drum. It was like a community theater production of *Hair* and I loved it. A strange sense of direction kicked in and I walked right to Celestina's dorm with no problem at all.

Her room was everything I'd dreamed mine would be. It was bright and cheerful, with air-conditioning and windows that looked onto Washington Square Park. She had a roommate who seemed sweet, and they had loft beds with desks underneath them with fun little lamps and corkboards above them. It was a dorm room dream. Celestina told me all about her first week at NYU—her classes and the people she had met, the teachers she loved, the boys she didn't like. She talked pretty much nonstop for two hours without once asking me a single question. I would later come to know this (and see it in myself) as a solid tell that someone is an actor. Somehow we can be completely self-centered yet give the listener the impression they are in on the fun. I didn't care. I was thrilled to be with people, and to feel like I'd been welcomed somewhere.

Celestina kicked me out after a couple hours because she had a Voice and Speech class in the morning. It all sounded so academic and artsy. We said our good-byes and I left. Once outside, I realized it was later than I'd thought, close to 11 p.m., and dark. I started back toward the subway certain of my way, but I must have made a wrong turn somewhere because before I knew it I was IN Washington Square Park.

I knew this wasn't right. I hadn't been this way before. Or had I? "The city is a grid, the city is a grid," I kept telling myself, unaware that it is most definitely not a grid below 14th Street. *I'll just go back to Celestina's dorm and start again,* I decided. *But which way was it?* It was at this point I realized there was no one else around. There are always people around in New York, so this felt odd. A young-ish man walked up behind me and mumbled, "Smoke? Smoke?" I continued to walk. "Coke? Coke?" I walked faster, so did he. "No, thank you!" I said. He walked away.

I felt like I was back on track now, that I was starting to figure out where the train was. Another man approached me. "What are you looking for? Coke?" Having grown up watching *Miami Vice*, I knew he wasn't talking about pop. (That's Midwestern for "soda.") "No, thank you!" I said again. This was getting ridiculous. I saw some drunk students weaving around across the street from me, shouting and laughing. *Maybe I should just ask them where the subway is?* Just then, one of them vomited on the sidewalk while his friends laughed at him.

Another man approached me. "Smoke? Smoke?"

"No!" I shouted. I felt like I was in a drug-infused opening number of *Oliver!*

And then, a miracle . . . a taxi appeared with its vacant light on. I stuck my arm out and the cab stopped. Just like in the movies! "57th and Lexington, please!" I belted. And off we went. The cab smelled like an armpit mixed with an ashtray, but I didn't care. I rolled down both windows and let the breeze come through. I looked around the city as we sped uptown. I could see that there was so much life happening everywhere. A woman getting off from work, waiting for the bus. A group of businessmen stumbling out of a bar. A young couple laughing and holding hands crossing the street. So many people I didn't know, who didn't know me. How would I fit into this world? It seemed so crowded already. Was there space for me? I felt lost and scared.

I wanted to go to my parents' hotel and tell them this was a mistake. *I should go home to Nebraska,* I thought. *I'll come back in a couple years when I've saved more money, when I can go to NYU instead of a school whose most famous alumna is Geraldine Ferraro, who, last time I checked, has never won any Tony Awards.* But even thinking these things felt wrong. I had to make a choice. I could be afraid of what was to come; I could panic about the decision I had made to move to New York with no contacts, no real friends, and no clue on how to get started. Or I could embrace it.

Sure, I didn't know anyone and my dreams of being on Broadway seemed light-years away, but isn't that how everyone starts here? Isn't that the beauty of New York? I didn't want to die of regret in Omaha. I wanted to try! Like Melanie Griffith in *Working Girl,* I could give myself a makeover and conquer this town, god damn it! I was Tootsie! I was Annie! I wasn't Coco from *Fame,* but I *was* Leroy from *Fame,* and I was going to rule that fucking school! Okay, maybe I was Danny, but still I felt calm all of a sudden. No more panic. No more sadness. Just calm. My heart had been racing moments before, but now, in the safety of a filthy cab, I felt okay. The lights of the city, the smells, the sounds, they all felt safe to me. I would find my place here. These people outside on the streets would be my friends, my neighbors. There *was* space for me—I would make sure of it.

I didn't know what was next. What school would be like,

who I would meet, how I would fit in. I didn't know that night that years later I would ask my parents about that trip and they would tell me that I seemed fine, capable, totally in control. That they felt awkward and in my way and wanted to give me space to set myself up. That as I was lost in Washington Square, they were in their hotel crying, together, because I was growing up and going away and they didn't know how to help this very ambitious son of theirs. I also didn't know that somehow this distance between us would actually make me and my dad closer. That there *would* be regular phone calls and stories told and thoughts shared in a way that we never could face-to-face. I didn't know how my mother, who seemed so frightened by this city, would fall in love with it too.

I didn't know that night how many romances this town would give me. The friends I would make, the fights I would get into. I didn't know about the jobs I would have, both the fantastic and the miserable, or how or when I would get to Broadway. I didn't know any of this. It was just the beginning. And I was ready for anything.

Be Loud

HOW DO I GET STARTED HERE? THAT WAS THE BIG question. I didn't know anyone except for other students, and I had zero clue how to get closer to my dream of being on Broadway. All I knew was what had worked in Omaha. Maybe if I just did that again, I could find success here. I mean, New York was basically just a bigger Omaha, *right*? I really had no choice but to try; I was convinced that a life on stage was my destiny.

I have been a shameless entertainer ever since I was a little kid. Singing and dancing in front of people, telling stories, trying to get people to laugh—I loved them all. But I didn't have a word for my need to perform then; "actor" wasn't a part of my vocabulary yet. Remember that game MASH you played as a kid? The one where you would write down different visions of your future: your job, your spouse, your car? Then you would continuously draw a spiral until someone said "Stop!"—at which point you'd use some nonsensical, child logic to figure out which future would come true? I never said "actor" in that game. I usually said "doctor" or "news anchor." (For what it's worth, I always said "Michelle Pfeiffer" or "Lisa Whelchel" for my wife. I also said "Lamborghini" for my car even though I really had no clue what that was.)

Even though I had seen my sister Becky in high school productions of *West Side Story* and *Fiddler on the Roof*—both productions were all Catholic, all white, and filled with lots of questionable accents—I had never imagined myself up on stage with her. The actors were all in their teens, I was a tiny child! I figured I would have to wait until I was older to have my turn.

Then came the day when my Catholic grade school, Our Lady of Lourdes, took a field trip to the Emmy Gifford Children's Theater, Omaha's premier (and only) children's theater. My class saw a production of *Frankenstein*, and there was a little boy my age in it. Suddenly an intense envy sank in. I had always been jealous of Ricky Schroder on *Silver Spoons*. Both of Ricky Schroder, *the actor*, getting to be the center of attention like that, and of Ricky Stratton, *the character*, and the fact that he had an indoor fucking train. But that life seemed insanely out of reach. I couldn't even begin to imagine what it would take to be the star of a television show or where to buy that kind of train. But who in the hell was this kid on stage at the Emmy Gifford? If there was going to be an Omaha Ricky, it was going to be *me*.

My parents regularly attended shows at our local community theater and *both* dinner theaters in town, so I figured my mom might know how I could break into the Omaha theater scene. I asked her how that kid got to be in that show, and she told me that the theater held "tryouts" and listed them in the *Omaha World Herald*'s LIVING! section. (It is still called the LIVING! section to this day.) I started scouring the Sunday paper for these "tryouts" and was regularly disappointed by the results. A community theater production of *Who's Afraid of Virginia Woolf?* I had never heard of it, but there should be a child in that, right? No such luck. The following week, tryouts for *One Flew Over the Cuckoo's Nest.* Surely that was a children's show? Nope. But then, after weeks of looking, I found it . . . *Oliver!* It was the jackpot of children's shows: basically all children, and boy children at that. Maybe I could just sign up for this one? There couldn't be *that* many boys who wanted to do theater. This was my chance to be Ricky.

I told my mother the good news. After reading the requirements in the ad, she explained that I would need to sing for the audition and I would need to bring something called "sheet music" for the piano player. Okay. I went to our piano, which no one in the house played, and riffled through the piano bench, where, for some reason, we had a lot of sheet music. I think my mother hoped that just by having it in the house, some musical ability might seep into our brains. We had *The Hits of Barry Manilow.* I considered "Copacabana," but it didn't seem quite right for an orphan. "The Theme from *Ice Castles*"? Solid choice, but would it be as effective without ice skates? And then I found it, shoved in the bottom of the bench: "Getting to Know You" from *The King and I.* It was perfect! They didn't know me; I was introducing myself to them. Slam dunk. My dad had shown me the movie years before, and I had completely fallen in love with it. I thought Deborah Kerr was the most beautiful woman I had ever seen, and I got a funny feeling down there when Yul Brynner dragged her around the dance floor without his shirt on. This was it. This was going to be my song and I was going to be in *Oliver!* at the Emmy Gifford Children's Theater. I told my mother and she agreed to take me to the audition. I'm sure she was thrilled that I was showing interest in anything besides watching hours of TV all day and telling her how bored I was.

I practiced my song again and again alone in the bathroom, when I was certain no one could hear me. I thought it would be perfectly okay to perform it with accompaniment for the first time at the tryout itself. Later that week we drove to the theater and much to my horror, it was packed with little boys who also wanted to be in *Oliver!* They all knew each other and were laughing and talking, they all had better hair, and they were all carrying binders filled with their sheet music. I, on the other hand, had brought along the entire "You Play the Hits of *The King and I*" book. *Stupid, Andy, stupid!* I thought.

As we walked in, a woman handed me a form with all sorts of information to fill in: age, height, weight, hair color, eye color, and at the bottom, a large space to write in "Past Experience." I panicked. Do I write down my re-creation of *Grease 2* in my garage? The lip-synced "A Boy Like That" my sister Natalie and I did in our living room when no one else was home? All of a sudden those didn't seem like legitimate productions. Did I have ANY experience to share? Sensing my agita, my mother said, "You can leave it blank. That's okay." I refused to listen to her. *I can't leave it blank. I must have some experience!* I racked my brain. *What the hell was that show I had to do in the first grade called? It was for an assembly or something, something about birds or I don't know, insects?* I quickly wrote down, "The Birds and The Flowers and The Bees."

My mother frowned. "What the hell is that?"

"It's the show we did in Sister Idalia's class three years ago."

"It is?" she asked doubtfully.

Damn it, Mother! Just go with me here!

"Are you sure, Andy?"

"Yes!" I said.

"Okay, then . . ."

I handed in my slightly false résumé, and the woman at the check-in table said we could have a seat in the theater. As we walked in, the gravity of the situation hit me. All of the other boys would be watching my audition, and there were hundreds of them. Okay, there were probably fifty, but they might as well have filled a stadium. We sat down, and my mother, picking up on my terror, said, "Are you sure you want to do this?"

"Yes!" I shot back. What I meant was "Fuck no!" but the words came out wrong. We settled in and watched little boy after little boy get on stage and belt out song after song. They all seemed amazing. Where in God's name were these children coming from? Why could everyone sing? No one sang at my grade school. I mean, we did in church, but that didn't count. These kids were singing like they were on *Star Search*.

I was beginning to think that maybe my mother and I should just slip out the back, and then they said it, "Andy Rannells, you are next!" I stood up. "Be loud" was my mother's final bit of advice. I walked onto the stage and gave the piano player my music. I remember very little about the thirty seconds of singing that followed, except that I had the feeling it wasn't going well and that I couldn't quite produce sound. I could barely hear myself over the piano. I finished and grabbed my music and practically ran off the stage. I could feel that my face was red and hot, and I wanted to cry immediately. When I got to my mother, she said, "I couldn't hear you."

We got into our Dodge Caravan and she softened. "That was very brave, Andy. I'm proud of you." I was devastated. I didn't want to be brave, I wanted to be Oliver. She tried to be helpful: "You know they teach classes at the Emmy Gifford Theater, too. Maybe that would be a good way to get started." *Classes?! I don't want to take classes! I want to be rewarded for my natural star power!* But I knew my mom was right. I needed help. This was going to be hard.

Needless to say, I did not get cast in *Oliver!* However, I got a glimmer of a feeling while on that stage. Even though standing up there had not gone well, as terrifying as it was it felt oddly familiar. I wasn't fully comfortable, but I knew I could be. I wanted to stay longer. And there was something else—the smell of the stage, it was dust and wood and something vaguely chemical that was instantly comforting. It was like I remembered that smell even though I was certain I had never smelled it before.

After a few weeks passed, I decided my mother was right: Classes would be the way to go. I asked her to sign me up and she did. I started going every Saturday, and eventually I got more and more confident. I liked it. I felt good there. I was finding out what my interests really were and I was finally feeling like I had a "thing." My brother had sports, my sisters had dance classes, I had theater.

A year later there was another audition. This time it was for *The Snow Queen.* I only knew the story from Shelley Duvall's *Faerie Tale Theatre* on TV, and honestly, Lee Remick scared the hell out of me, so it was not my favorite, but this was a chance to redeem myself. I asked my mom if I could audition, and once again she said yes. This time there was no singing, which was a relief.

The day of the audition came, and I was ready to get back on that stage. I was eleven years old and I had overcome whatever PTSD had remained from *Oliver!* There was just one problem: My mother forgot about the audition and was at a dance class with my youngest sister, Natalie. My father was out with my brother Dan, my sister Julie was off being a candy striper, or at least hanging out at a hospital for some reason, and my oldest sister, Becky, was off doing whatever college kids did during the day when they were stuck living at home. I was alone in our house losing my goddamned mind. This was supposed to be my comeback, and I was being foiled by everyone else's schedule.

I remember pacing around the house, looking out the windows, willing someone, anyone with a driver's license, to come home. It was getting dark out, and I knew the auditions were coming to a close. I nearly started crying, and then I felt foolish. Who was I kidding? I wasn't going to get it anyway. I was terrible at this. Yes, I took a class, but so did a lot of kids. Who did I think I was? Lance Polokov? (He was the boy who was cast as Oliver. He seemed far too tall for the role in my opinion.) *Forget it*, I thought, *I give up*. I turned on *Head of the Class* and decided to call it a night.

Just then, Becky came home. She could tell something was off about me and asked what was wrong. I didn't want to get into it, but I slowly told her about the audition. There must have been alarm or sadness in my voice, because she said, "Let's go."

"Really?"

"Yes, let's hurry."

I couldn't believe it. Before I had time to think about it, we were in her Monte Carlo speeding to the theater. We ran in and I asked if it was too late to try out. The woman at the desk said they were just finishing up.

"But he can still go, right?" Becky asked.

The woman looked at her watch. "I guess so. But you'll have to go right now. Here is the scene." This was happening. I took the scene and quickly read it as I walked into the theater.

There was no one in there except the director, a seemingly old man who was, in actuality, probably thirty. He was standing at the foot of the stage, straightening up papers, when he saw me. "One more? Okay, then. Come on up." I got up on the stage, too shocked to be nervous. "What's your name?" the director asked.

My mother's "I couldn't hear you" came back to haunt me, and I would be damned if I made the same mistake again. "Andy Rannells," I yelled, even though he was four feet away from me.

He smiled at me. "Okay. Let's read the scene. You'll be Noah and I'll be Greta."

I was standing on the stage, there was light on my face, and I could smell that smell again. *This is it.* I proceeded to shout the entire scene at the director. I had no idea what I was saying, but it was LOUD. That glimmer of a feeling I had gotten at my first audition came back to me, but this time stronger and clearer. I felt in control. I felt like I had something to say and the skill to say it. I felt like . . . I might be good. We finished the scene. He smiled again. "Thank you for coming in, Andy. They saved the best for last."

I walked, or rather floated, off the stage. Becky was standing in the back of the theater. "Great job, Andy! I could hear you all the way back here." I didn't have the words to tell Becky thank you, so I just hugged her and tried not to cry. I didn't care about getting in the show anymore. I had just wanted a chance to redeem myself, and I did. But you know what? I did get that show. I was cast in my first real Emmy Gifford Children's Theater production. I was not cast as Noah, the lead, nor was I given a single line. Instead, I was essentially an extra who ran across the stage a couple times. But I was living my dream.

I continued to take classes. There were "Dialects from Around the World," "Basic Stage Combat," and my favorite, "Scenes from *Crimes of the Heart*: Ages 9 to 14." I took them all and I loved them all. And there were more shows, too. I played the pivotal role of "Lurvey the Farmhand" in *Charlotte's Web*, I was a very tall Oompa Loompa in *Charlie and the Chocolate Factory*, and I played a Celtic warrior in a politically correct version of *Peter Pan*. (The theater knew they shouldn't have "Indians" as scripted, so they changed it to "Celtic Warriors." It was the year *Braveheart* came out. Celts were all the rage.)

Soon I found myself outgrowing children's theater. I wanted more. I wanted . . . *dinner* theater. Dinner theater may have fallen out of fashion in most parts of the country by the early nineties, but not in Nebraska. It was still very popular and a real date-night destination for many couples, including my parents. They would go a few times a year, getting all dressed up and then coming home late at night smelling of booze and cigarette smoke. It all seemed so glamorous. There were several in town and I felt certain that I was ready to graduate to this next level.

I got my chance at the Firehouse Dinner Theater, in a production of *On Golden Pond*. (The Firehouse Dinner Theater was especially swanky; they served Grasshoppers and you got to keep the glass they came in.) There was only one kid in that show, a character named Billy, and I got the part. He was Jane Fonda's bratty stepson in the movie, and I made the bold choice to copy Doug McKeon's performance exactly. It worked. I was a hit! A few months later I won the Omaha Theater Arts Guild Award for Best Youth Actor. *See you later, children's theater,* I thought. *I'm on my way to the top!*

I continued to work my way through the Omaha theater scene, and by the time I reached senior year of high school, I had been in a production at nearly every theater in town. I would set my sights on a place and will myself into one of their shows. It worked every time. Except for a production of *Marvin's Room* at the Omaha Community Playhouse. Josh Perilo got the part of Hank. To my eye, he seemed far too old for the role.

So when I arrived in New York, I was hopeful that my Omaha theater formula would work. But how did one find out about auditions for Broadway shows? Was there a section in the *New York Times*? I couldn't find "Auditions" or the LIVING! section in any paper. I heard someone at school say that they had heard that if you took your headshot to the theater and left it for the stage manager, they would tell you when they were having auditions. That seemed easy enough.

I had a headshot that a wedding photographer in Omaha had taken. I was wearing a black dress shirt from Younkers department store and an oversized plaid blazer from Structure, and I had styled my hair to look like Zack Morris's on *Saved by the Bell*. In other words, I was nailing it.

My résumé consisted of all my Omaha credits ranked from largest role to smallest. Feeling good, I packed up my headshots and walked into Times Square. Though I wasn't certain that I could find the stage door to any theater, I was determined to make the effort. The first show I went to that day was *Rent*, which was also the first show I had ever seen on Broadway. It was my favorite and I listened to it constantly. I was sure I could be a Mark if given the chance. I went to the theater and marched up to the front door. This was too easy! I rang the bell and a gruff man answered. "Can I help you?" he asked.

"I'm just leaving this for the stage manager."

"Great," he said, before grabbing the manila envelope and slamming the door. Not exactly the warm embrace I was looking for, but efficient. Okay. One down! Who's next? I worked my way uptown. *Phantom of the Opera*? Why not? "I'm leaving this for the stage manager, please." Done. *Miss Saigon*? Hell yes! "For the stage manager!" Done. *The Life*? I could be a hooker! "This is for the stage manager." Done. *Smokey Joe's Cafe*? There's a white guy on the poster and that might as well be me! "This is for the stage manager." Done. Soon I was out of headshots and exhausted but exhilarated from strutting around Times Square. This plan had to work. Why wouldn't it? All my other plans had worked. Now I just had to wait.

So I waited. And waited. And waited. Weeks went by and I heard nothing. I was crushed. I worried that I had done something wrong, but I wasn't even sure who to ask. At this point in my college life, all I could do was turn to my first group of friends, a trio of girls from Long Island—two Lizzies and a Samantha—who knew everything and cared about nothing (and who would only last for another week or so, until I realized I had better, nicer options). They seemed fancy in a *Dance Party USA* way, and their accents were both grating and intriguing. Samantha even had a manager! "He wants me to focus on film and TV," she used to say all the time. I'm pretty certain he was her uncle and she was fucking him, but a manager is a manager.

I had decided to tell no one about my headshot/stage door tour—I didn't want anyone stealing the idea—but out of desperation to share my disappointment, I told Samantha. She laughed in my face. "Are you serious? I'm sure they are all in a trash can." *Could that be true?* I wondered. *Am I the laughingstock of Broadway right now? Is every theater making fun of my headshot? My résumé? My blazer?* I felt disgusting and sad, and I hated Samantha for telling me this. I quickly changed the topic. Our friendship would only last a few more days. I stopped speaking to her entirely when she told me I was too gay to be on *Dawson's Creek*.

Then, one night, I came home from class and I had a message on my answering machine from my mother in Omaha:

"Hi, Andy. Just calling to say, 'Hi.' I also wanted to tell you that Jean Pulhachek passed away. Apparently she choked on some chicken in a Chinese chicken salad at her niece's confirmation party. Sad. Oh, also, you got a call from someone from *Rent* that you have a tryout on Thursday to be an angel. I think that's what the gal said. I wrote it down. Call me later."

What in holy hell was she talking about? Why did *Rent* call her? Was this a prank? Did Samantha do this to get even with me for telling people she was sleeping with her manager who was also her uncle? Then I remembered that I had never changed the number on my résumé; it was still my parents' number in Omaha. I was leaving the fate of my Broadway dreams to my mother. How many offers had I missed these past weeks? I called my mom immediately. "I just got your message! What's happening?!"

"Well, the chicken got caught in her trachea, and no one knew she was even choking until she passed out. But even then, they just thought she was napping. It's all so sad."

"Not that part! The *Rent* part!"

"Oh! Sure! You have a tryout on Thursday for an angel. The gal wants you to call her back."

I didn't have the emotional strength to explain to my mother that it wasn't for AN angel, it was for THE Angel and *Rent* was the biggest show on Broadway! I took the number, listened for a few more minutes about the funeral arrangements for a woman I was certain I had never met, and then I danced around my dorm room like a maniac. My plan did work after all! Fuck you, Samantha!

I didn't fully realize at the time just how remarkable this really was. I had not followed protocol at all. Dropping off headshots at the stage door wasn't really a thing, it was just something I didn't know any better *not* to do. But it worked. It was too late to call the casting director that night, so I just had to wait until morning. My mind raced with possibilities. I didn't really see myself as Angel, but I was flexible. I could do that. I would have to learn how to drum. I wondered where I could find some empty buckets to jam on.

The next day I phoned, and just as my mother had said, I was being called in to audition to replace Angel in the Broadway production of *Rent*. The audition was in two days and I would need to prepare "Today 4 U" and "I'll Cover You." I already knew both songs and was prepared to sing the whole score if need be. The woman from casting then said, "Where can we fax you the sides?" Faxing! Sides! Show business! I had the sides faxed to the front desk of my dorm, and then casually wandered through the building waving them around, praying someone would ask me what I was up to. "What am I doing? Oh, I'm just getting ready for my *Rent* audition on Thursday. I have this material that was FAXED to me just now. I really should be going. It's going to be a *lot* of prep work."

The day arrived and I was ready. I skipped my classes, put on my new Calvin Klein carpenter jeans and a ribbed T-shirt from the Gap, and waltzed into that casting office ready to fulfill my destiny. The room was packed with young Latino men all dressed in various stages of drag. *Oh my god.* I had not even thought about that as an option. *Why didn't I put on some lipstick or something?* Then part two of the reality of this audition set in: Angel was Latino. I was not Latino. I was the opposite of Latino. It hadn't occurred to me that this might be a problem. (Our most recent version of *West Side Story* in Omaha had featured a blond Maria. And no one cared.) *I can still make this work,* I told myself. I took a seat and avoided eye contact with anyone. Through the wall, I could clearly hear the other men singing their faces off and everyone sounded great. After listening to "I'll Cover You" on a loop for about twenty minutes, I was called into the room. *Here it is,* I thought. *My first Broadway audition.*

There was one young woman behind a table looking at headshots and résumés. I saw mine on the table. She picked it up. "Are you Andrew?" (By that point, I had started going by my full name. I was in New York now.)

"Yes, I am Andrew Rannells."

"Thanks for coming in, Andrew. Are you ready to sing?"

"Yes, I am!"

I was going to hit her with all the Latin heat I could muster.

"Before you sing," she said, "can I ask what your mix is?"

My mix? My *mix*? What did *that* mean? She could see I was puzzled by her, what I now know is illegal, question.

"Like where are your ancestors from?"

"OH! Poland and Ireland."

She stared at my photo for a long time.

"So you're not Asian?"

"No. Not Asian."

Was I supposed to be Asian? Did my mother tell them the Chinese chicken salad story and they got confused? The woman stared at me and then at the photo and then at me, and then finally said, "I guess you can sing anyway."

I planted my feet and I belted out "I'll Cover You" as best I could, trying not to be distracted by the fact that I was swimming in an ethnically confused haze. I finished the song and she gave me a half smile. "You've got some real pipes. Thanks for coming in." That was it. I didn't even get to sing the second song I'd prepared.

I walked out of the building confused, disappointed, and

exhausted from the adrenaline crash that quickly set in. *Did I blow it? Should I be mad? Should I be sad? It was supposed to go better than that.* Then it hit me; I was back at the beginning again. All that work in Omaha didn't mean anything. I would have to start over. Did I have the strength to do that again? It seemed like a lifetime since I'd blown my *Oliver!* audition, and yet the feeling was exactly the same. I felt so far away from everything I wanted.

I decided to skip my other classes that day, and I just wandered around the city. I walked up to Times Square and weaved my way through the Broadway theaters. Their doors were right there, but I didn't know how to open them. As I walked around, I realized that I wasn't feeling the exact disappointment I felt after *Oliver!* because this time I was feeling disappointed in New York. I was starting from the bottom, but at least I was living in New York now. It's not like I lost the role of Angel to Lance Polokov. He was nowhere in sight! That in itself felt like an accomplishment.

A couple weeks later *Rent* announced their new Angel. It was Wilson Cruz from TV's *My So-Called Life*. I weirdly felt relieved. I couldn't compete with Rickie! But at least now I had a story. I had auditioned for my first Broadway show. My New York career had started, and this time I was a little bit ahead, because I knew the secret to my past success: Be patient. Be persistent. Be loud.

A New Me for New York

BEFORE ACTUALLY MOVING TO NEW YORK, I VISited twice. The first time was during my senior year of high school when I had an opportunity to travel with a bunch of people I did community theater with. The median age of the group was probably fifty, so at eighteen I guess my parents thought I would be safe and mostly bored. I was determined to *fit in* in New York City. I always felt on the outside in Omaha and just assumed that it was because I didn't ultimately belong there. Even though I had never been to New York, I knew it was where I was meant to be. I refused to be wrong about that.

We had tickets to several shows, including the biggest hit of that year, *Rent*, and I could barely control my excitement. I did have one major fear however: What was I going to wear? I had a feeling that I was going to need to adjust my appearance to blend in in New York. I talked to my mother about my concern, and much to my joy and surprise, she agreed to take me shopping. Charlotte and I were, and are, very close, and she knew how important this trip was for me. I will always love her for understanding that.

And so we set off for the Crossroads Mall to buy me some snazzy outfits for my big trip to the Big Apple. We picked out slacks and blazers and ties and dress shirts. Drawing on her own teen model days, she showed me how to mix and match pieces so that I could get away with packing less but still looking like I was wearing a whole new outfit every night. This was 1996, so please keep in mind that men's fashion, particularly in Nebraska, was still all very oversized. If it helps you understand this, at eighteen I bought the same size blazer I wear at thirty-nine. And I'm about fifty pounds heavier. But it didn't matter! Charlotte made sure I was dressed at the height of fashion. She made me into a nineties version of George Peppard from *Breakfast at Tiffany's*, and I loved every thread of it.

That first trip to New York City was a dream come true. We saw *Rent, The Life, Titanic, Sunset Boulevard, When Pigs Fly,* and *Gross Indecency.* I didn't see any landmarks or famous tourist destinations, and I barely left Midtown, but I couldn't have been happier. Because I was surrounded by much older people, I never got carded in restaurants. Waiters probably assumed that I was either a white Emmanuel Lewis or being held captive by a bunch of Midwestern theater queens. In any event, they all agreed I deserved a drink. I think I drank a bottle of Merlot at every meal. And not for nothing, my outfits were a hit. I was looking great and feeling handsome. I was really able to picture myself living in New York City— dining at fine restaurants, seeing shows, walking the streets with purpose and a solid sense of direction, all while wearing a pleated pant, an oversized olive blazer, a black dress shirt, and a bold, bordering on ethnic print tie.

Then, on one of our last nights in New York, we had dinner near Lincoln Center. As we started to walk home, me strutting proudly, albeit drunkenly, in my Brandon Walsh tribute attire, I saw them. Students just a few years older than me leaving Juilliard. There was a large group of them parading across the plaza at Lincoln Center, illuminated by the fountain behind them. They all looked so . . . *cool.* Some had leather jackets and tight jeans, others wore trench coats and berets, and everything everyone wore was black. *So chic.* Most were smoking cigarettes and they all were laughing together, probably at some inside joke about how sophisticated they all were. As if in slow motion, I had a moment of seeing them in all their glory and then assessing my group in all their . . . Midwestern-ness. There were BeDazzled tops and wide-legged trousers, bolo ties and silk shirts. And me. Me at eighteen trying to look forty. I was embarrassed for me.

I liked most of the people I was traveling with. They were nice people, good people, but they didn't have dreams of leaving Omaha. At least not anymore. They fit in perfectly where we lived, but I wanted out. That was the moment I knew I had to *really* change. This was a bigger project than I had realized.

My next trip to New York was scheduled for three months later, when I would return to audition for colleges. I would be coming alone because my parents had decided it would be a good chance for me to practice living there alone. I think it was probably a test my father got my mother to agree to, hoping that the experience would be so terrifying that I would come straight home and give up this nonsense dream of living in New York City. (That said, given that my dad's conception of New York was largely shaped by *Homicide: Life on the Street,* I'm also a little disturbed that he wanted to give me that risky a test.) But I was ready, damn it.

This time, though, I wanted to switch up my look. I wanted to dress like those artsy, edgy Juilliard students. But I knew I couldn't ask Charlotte to take me shopping again. I couldn't hurt her feelings that way, mainly because I was, and still am to this day, scarred by an event that took place when I was in the fourth grade.

Picture it: Omaha, 1988. I was going to perform in Dickens in the Market, an annual holiday event during which small Omaha children dressed up like Dickensian orphans and begged for money while singing Christmas carols in a neighborhood known as the "Old Market." It had cobblestone streets, and I imagined it was the closest thing to London we could get in Omaha. Everyone was in charge of his or her own costume, and while some people rented costumes, other mothers would make theirs. Charlotte said she would make one for me, and for some reason or other, I hated it. I thought it didn't look *Oliver!* enough. I had a full-tilt breakdown alone in my room. My brother Dan tried to comfort me, but when I started blaming our mother, he quickly came to her defense. This enraged me even more, and I remember shouting at him, "She couldn't have just rented one! She didn't even care that much! She's lazy! She's a lazy mom!" As the words came out of my mouth, I could sense Charlotte behind me in the doorway of the bedroom. She was crying, and she said, "I'm sorry you think I'm lazy, Andy. I tried." Well, holy fuck. I had never felt shame like that in all of my ten years on Earth. I immediately started crying harder, this time for a good reason. I tried apologizing, but it was too late. She was crying, I was crying. To this day I have never felt so bad in my life. And I've done some shitty things. Charlotte remade the costume, I thanked her profusely, and we never spoke of it again. I am aware that was a real fucking tangent, but (a) it seemed to make sense in my head, and (b) I needed to publicly apologize to my mother for that incident. I'm sorry, Charlotte. I'm sorry for acting like such an ungrateful little dick.

All that to say that there was no way in hell I was going to tell my mother I needed new "looks" months after she had bought me new "looks." I would have to figure it out myself. Based on the new mix 'n' match skill Charlotte had taught me, I decided to take stock of what I *did* have. I pulled everything that was black out of my closet and drawers. I had more than I'd expected. There was a turtleneck, some T-shirts, a dress shirt, a blazer, and some pants that I had stolen from my brother even though he was taller than I was. (I wasn't aware of *sizing* yet, just *content*.)

I thought about the Juilliard kids I had seen. What was I missing? Oh, right. Leather! Luckily, my father had a leather trench coat that had lived in the back of his closet for decades. He must have bought it in the seventies after seeing *Shaft* and never actually worn it. I decided it was perfect for my trip. I asked my father, and surprisingly, Ron said yes. (He was often annoyed at my obsession with what I was wearing and how I would be perceived. He would say, "No one is looking at you, Andy." I knew he was right. But I wanted to prove him wrong.)

There was still one thing missing from my second stab at a cool New Yorker outfit, and I knew exactly where to find it. I went to the community dinner theater where I had done many shows and snuck into the costume closet. After rummaging around, I found it: a tattered box marked BERETS. Why was there a whole box of berets? Who knows? My guess was a long-ago production of *Gigi*. I didn't care. I needed that hat to complete my look. I shoved a beret into my pocket and snuck back out. Everything was ready for my audition trip.

I arrived alone at Newark Airport. I would be staying with a girl named Laura who had been the Anybodys to my Baby John in *West Side Story* a few years earlier. She was a freshman at Marymount Manhattan College, which was one of a handful of programs I would be auditioning for. She told me to take the bus to Port Authority, and then from Port Authority, take the subway to her dorm on the Upper West Side. I was terrified that I would miss a step on this multi-step adventure and end up being sex trafficked, proving my mother right. But I remained calm. I could figure this out. On my way out of the airport I decided I should buy some cigarettes as one final prop. I thought it would finish the look and make me seem "tough."

For those of you trying to envision this final fashion project, let me help. It went like this: black boots from a store at Crossroads Mall called "Savage," black jeans from the Gap, a black turtleneck (probably my father's from JCPenney), my dad's black leather trench coat, my precious beret, black-rimmed John Lennon sunglasses I found at a thrift store in the Old Market, and now . . . a cigarette, not being inhaled. I thought I looked like a beatnik, but in reality I looked like a teenager playing a blind hobo in the seventies.

When I arrived at Laura's dorm, she took one look at me and I could immediately tell I had gone too far. I wasn't very close with Laura, but I did confide in her my fears about not fitting in. She was sweet, and in a tone that could only be described as ridiculously condescending, she said, "Andy, you don't have to wear ALL black. I've been here for six months. I know." She seemed so wise; I had to trust her. I immediately started reimagining all of the clothes I had brought. It was demoralizing.

I also started wondering when I had made wardrobe mistakes in my past. Should I not have tried wearing that painter's cap in the sixth grade? What about the puff-painted sweatshirts I'd made? The Bart Simpson pins on my satin-y baseball jacket? I had always been trying to fit in. *Trying* was the key word. Maybe I just needed to stop trying so hard. (P.S. The following year Laura got a full-blown perm, but she referred to it as "a body wave." I realized she didn't know as much as she thought she did.)

After finally moving to New York for college, I decided to give myself a break and allow my own look to come to me. I started taking note of people who looked great to me. I wanted to look cool, but I also wanted to be authentic and be honest about who I was. I was a nineteen-year-old guy from Nebraska. I wasn't supposed to look like I was born in New York. I wasn't.

There were still several mishaps over the years though, including:

- **The Fifth Member of Third Eye Blind:** This involved a leather wrist cuff and short tees with graphics like "The Ramones" or "D.A.R.E." over long-sleeve tees.
- **Hamptons Realness:** This misstep stemmed from the fact that I had never been to the Hamptons. I was con-

vinced that people there wore khakis and very fitted ox-
fords and penny loafers. I looked like a slutty Kinko's
employee.

- **The Robert Redford Tribute:** This involved blond highlights, thick turtlenecks, and a camel-colored wool
  trench coat.

- *Titanic*-**era Leonardo DiCaprio's Gay Brother:** I would
  make my hair extra floppy, and sometimes slightly wet,
  and wear a white dress shirt with a wide-legged dress
  pant I stole from the dinner theater and a pair of ill-
  fitting suspenders.

- **My Own Private Idaho, or "I Didn't Realize That I
  Looked Like I Was Asking to Be Abducted":** Perhaps my most humiliating look, this featured a child's
  "Large" white T-shirt underneath . . . wait for it . . .
  denim overalls from the Gap.

I don't regret any of my "looks," especially the fails. I
think that I had to pass through all of them to figure out
who I was, or at least who I wasn't. Plus, I immediately had
the sense that while I hadn't quite found what I was looking
for, I was definitely on the right track. Sure, maybe I wasn't
as cool as those Juilliard kids I had seen, but honestly, who's
to say they were cool in the first place? They could have been
real assholes for all I knew. And besides, I hadn't escaped the
sea of BeDazzled sweaters in Omaha just to jump into an
ocean of black separates in New York; I had come to transform into someone new. And if that was true, I figured that
I should probably work on my personality rather than worry
about how my beret fit.

Oh, but I did finally develop a tip that is pretty helpful: You can always achieve inspiration for any event by looking at outfits James Dean or Cary Grant wore and trying to replicate them. It usually works. Occasionally you look like you are going to a Halloween party, but it's worth the risk.

The 40-Year-Old and
the Virgin

LESS THAN A MONTH AFTER MOVING TO MY CELL
at the Allerton Hotel—I mean, my *dorm* at the Allerton Hotel—it was nearly uninhabitable. The building's walls
were crumbling, the pipes were rusted, there were roaches everywhere; it was so bad that the *New York Times* even wrote a
story about it. I'll admit that I was slightly oblivious to many
of these issues. I just figured that this was New York living.
As long as there weren't police body outlines in the lobby, I
was good. But other students, and their parents, disagreed.
The combination of angry parents and bad press encouraged
Marymount to move us all out of the Allerton House of
Structural Horrors.

The school's administrators were instantly set into a mad
panic to find us all a new place to live, and they found it in
another old hotel, this one in Brooklyn Heights. It was called
the St. George Hotel and was located right in the center of one
of the most charming, most quintessential Brooklyn Heights
blocks, just steps away from the Promenade. The building
was beautiful and newly renovated. The rooms were spacious
and filled with natural light. The only downside was that we
had to share rooms, and I had to pick a roommate quickly.
I chose a very quiet, very nice guy in my acting class named

Tom. I didn't know much about him, but he was sweet and, like me, also seemed a little out of place, so he was a good fit for me. We mostly didn't see each other, but some nights we would both stay in and watch *The Golden Girls* while eating whole pints of Ben & Jerry's ice cream. *This* felt like college. *This* was what I was missing.

It was here in Brooklyn Heights, during my second month of living on my own in a new city, that I finally found my footing. I knew which subways got me to school fastest. I knew which pizzeria in my neighborhood had the best pepperoni slices. I knew that Grace's Marketplace on the Upper East Side was stupidly overpriced, but that you could sometimes see Lena Horne shopping there if you were lucky. I felt like I belonged. In the way that only happens when you are nineteen, a few weeks away from Omaha felt like a lifetime.

Then one night, he just showed up. He had talked his way into my dorm; I think security assumed he was a parent. I was scared. I didn't want him there. Tom could tell that something was wrong. I lied and said everything was fine and that this man was just a man from my past in Omaha who was visiting, nothing more. The man said that he had no place to stay that night, that he had traveled all that way to see me and that he needed to stay with me. He wouldn't leave.

Let me back up and start by saying I *thought* I knew what I was doing. It was 1995, I was sixteen years old, and I thought I knew it all. I saw an opportunity and I decided to go for it. Sex seemed very far away. I didn't know any other gay teenagers in Omaha, so there was no one to experiment with. I figured I would have to wait until college. I guess

I could have had sex with some girl who didn't know any better, who didn't see that my affections lay elsewhere. But having a younger sister, I just kept thinking, *Would I want my sister to have this experience with someone who wasn't fully invested in her?* The answer was no.

So here I was, crawling out of my skin with manic sexual energy, getting a boner if someone walked past me too closely or there was even the suggestion of nudity or any kind of sexuality. I also happened to be spending a lot of time with adults in my community theater circle. Adults who were sexually active and who had none of the teenage hang-ups I did. And that is where I met him. He was a bit of a star in the local community theater scene. I had seen him on stage before and he was nice to me. He took an interest in me. That's what I wanted.

When he approached me and I felt like things were moving in a sexual direction, I just said yes. It started in his car. He used to drive me home from rehearsals, and one night, he put his hand on my leg and I didn't say no. We went from there. My hand eventually met his leg, and it was clear to both of us what game we were playing. It was so slow. It must have taken weeks for me to eventually work my hand higher, and to allow him to move his. I trusted him and I believed that this was safe and somehow blameless. Once a certain level of touching was reached, everything came together rather quickly.

It was the day of the Our Lady of Lourdes fall festival when we sealed the deal. I was volunteering with my parents at the Duck Pond booth at the festival. After a couple of hours of passing out stuffed animals, while simultaneously fantasizing about the most explicit sex acts that I could imagine, I snuck off and met him at his house. We talked about the usual things: local community theater politics, where I thought I might end up post–high school. Then we were kissing, which felt exciting and wrong, but exciting nonetheless. Clothes started to come off, and that felt even more wrong/exciting. I wasn't attracted to him, but it was a man's body and a mouth and I had never experienced either. *This might be your only chance,* I thought, so I relaxed. And it happened. Mouths and penises and feelings and panic, and before I knew it, it was over. It was on a couch and it smelled like incense and I loved and hated it.

So much pressure was put on this moment. I was supposed to love him, right? I was supposed to feel something. But I didn't. I felt shame and relief and a combination of feelings that probably everyone feels when they lose their virginity. I felt in control and out of control all at the same time. What I didn't expect were *his* feelings. I thought it was just about me. But he had other ideas. He wanted commitment, he wanted this to keep going. It should have ended there, on that sweaty afternoon, but it didn't. It continued sporadically and messily.

Cars.

Dressing rooms.

His house.

Rarely a bed.

Sometimes I would skip the last class of the day to meet him. Ironically, the class was "Moral Values." Catholic high school at its finest.

Another major factor in this mess was that he had a boyfriend who found out about our meetings. Rather than being concerned that his forty-year-old boyfriend was having sex with a sixteen-year-old, his boyfriend was mad at *me*. He blamed me for his lover's indiscretion. I was some Lolita who had lured him away. I felt guilty and wanted to say to this guy, "Hey, I don't want to date him. I don't love him. Please take him back. Please take him away." But this guy insisted on blaming me. And a big part of me didn't blame him for blaming me. I felt like I was responsible, after all. I was doing exactly what he said I was.

Eventually the boyfriend parked his car outside my house and just sat there. I talked to him—I told him to leave. He said that he was going to tell my parents, that he was going to tell *everyone* what I had done to him. I was terrified. For me to be forced out of the closet at this age, because of this man, was unimaginable. I couldn't have my parents find out I was gay this way. I knew that I would tell them one day, but not like this.

He finally drove away, but he came back another night. I was coming home from a high school dance and he was parked outside my parents' house. I approached him again and he asked if my parents were home. He wanted to talk to them.

"I'm going to tell them what a slut you are. How you ruined my life because you are such a whore."

Just then my brother Dan came home from his own night out. He saw me talking to this stranger in a car and asked what was going on. I pulled him aside and told him that this guy was crazy. That he thought I was having an affair with his boyfriend. His *boyfriend* of all things. I told my brother that I wanted him to leave. Dan was a few inches taller than I was and broad. He played rugby and looked tough. He walked up to the driver's side window and threatened this guy. He said if he didn't leave our house he would kick his ass. The boyfriend drove away. I thanked my brother; I didn't even try to explain anything, and he asked no questions. I was grateful and humiliated. I had gotten myself into a situation that I couldn't get out of, and I didn't want my family to be involved in my mistake. I was going to end it with this man. The sixteen-year-old would have to break up with the forty-year-old.

But he wouldn't let me do it. Weeks later, his boyfriend finally came to his senses and left him. Now the forty-year-old said he blamed me for everything. He said I had come on to him and that I had destroyed his relationship and left him with nothing. I couldn't leave him now, I couldn't leave him alone after what I had done to him. Then he told me he loved me. That he was IN love with me and that he wanted to be with me. That I owed it to him to at least try. He cried. I was disgusted by him, but I also felt terrible. What had I done to this man? Did I really destroy him? Did I really *make* him fall in love with me? I didn't know what to do, I didn't know what to say. So I said nothing. I did nothing.

I continued to have sex with this man but tried to avoid him as much as possible. I tried to make excuses about why I couldn't see him, but he would eventually wear me down and I would agree to spend time with him. I started to allow myself to like the sex. I tried to relax and to explore with him. I decided that I would do everything with him so that I had all my firsts out of the way before I left for college. I felt like

I was already damaged goods, I was already dirty, so what did it matter?

Months went by like this. A year. Finally, I was a senior in high school. I could see there was a perfect escape hatch on its way. My departure for college, for New York, meant escaping so many things now. It was starting to feel desperate, my escape. I needed it badly. A brief reprieve came in the form of the National Foundation for Advancement in the Arts, a highly competitive college scholarship program. Kids my age from all over the country—young actors, singers, dancers, musicians—were flown to Miami, Florida, to audition for scholarships. I was chosen as one of them from a VHS-taped audition I had sent in months earlier. I was thrilled. It was so validating and so encouraging. I was picked because I was a good enough actor to compete with kids from the most prestigious performing arts high schools in the country. It was exactly the boost I needed before moving to New York in the fall.

That's where I met Craig, a beautiful, beautiful dancer, who was exactly my age and from Chicago. The minute I saw him, I thought I was in love with him. Even though I knew that this relationship might only last the week, that Craig would go back to Chicago and I would go back to Omaha, I tried to luxuriate in every minute with him. I realized that I could have something romantic that felt right, that felt good and pure and not shameful or like an obligation. And he would also be moving to New York in the fall, so . . . who knew what could happen? Craig and I had one night together while the chaperones were distracted, or just generous. We had sex and I felt the closest thing I had felt to love in my life. It was all I had ever wanted, all that was missing. I tried not to think about my sullied past and focused on what my future could look like.

Earlier in the week, I had found myself in a circle of young people talking about what young people like to talk about: who was a virgin and who was not and who was gay and who was not. Not a conversation I was typically having in Omaha. I had opened up to this group of young strangers and told them about my "relationship" with the now forty-two-year-old. No one was as shocked as I had hoped or feared they would be. Some had similar stories. I felt relief and also sadness that we shared that experience.

One of these young people, another dancer, hadn't said anything, but he'd taken in this information about me. That night, my first and last night with Craig, we separated to pack our bags but agreed to meet up in an hour to be together again. In that hour, that dancer told Craig about my relationship with the older man in Omaha. He told him I was *dating* a forty-two-year-old. Craig was upset; he felt I had lied to him and I guess I had. Or at least avoided the truth. I tried to explain that I didn't love this man, that it was all a mistake, that I was trapped. But it was too late. Craig didn't forgive me, and he left, hurt and sad. I was furious at myself and my situation. The stench of this regrettable relationship had followed me all the way from home.

When I got back to Omaha, I vowed to end things with the forty-year-old once and for all. But again, there were tears and yelling and begging and pleading and threats and shouting, and again I did nothing. I still had a few months before I left home for New York. I would just have to be patient.

My head was a mess at this point. I felt confused, scared, lost. It was about this time that my mother asked me if something was going on between me and this older man. We were in the laundry room, folding something, socks maybe? I had a moment of relief, but also a moment of doubt. Was I being caught or freed? And then I almost said it. I almost said, "Yes, and I need it to stop. I need your help. Please." But instead I looked her in the eye and said, "No." She asked again and again I said, "No." And that was all. The moment passed. The window closed.

There was an adult outside of my family who saw what was happening and tried to help. One. Her name was Pam Carter, and she was my first serious acting teacher as a kid. (She taught "Scenes from *Crimes of the Heart*: Ages 9 to 14.") She had heard that something might be happening between me and this man, and she confronted us both. Her only mistake was that she confronted us together. I didn't feel like I could cling to her the way I wanted to. I couldn't say, "YES! Thank you!" Instead he did all the talking and was very defensive and very slippery, and somehow we got away from Pam. She talked to us both a couple more times, but it was always the same routine, always the same ending. Let me also add here that there was a big part of me that really believed I had chosen this. That I was in control as much as I was out of control. That I didn't need to be rescued (even though I wanted to be). I just wanted to leave Omaha and leave that man, the whole experience, behind me.

When I arrived in New York that August, I did just that. It was the beginning of me running from things I didn't want to acknowledge. I would become very good at that race as the weeks went on. It worked, I mostly forgot him. I mostly moved on.

Until he showed up at my dorm that night. All of the thoughts I had shoved down, that I thought I had left behind, were now in my doorway. My new location, my new clothes—none of it could protect me from what was standing in front of me. I didn't know what to do. I was afraid to make a scene. I wish now I would have. Instead, I folded. I let him stay. He slept in my dorm room twin bed while I slept on the floor. I refused to touch him. My poor roommate must have been so confused about what this man was doing in our room. I lay on the floor that night, nervous, but seething with anger that he had invaded my new life. That wasn't the way it was supposed to work. I was supposed to leave and he was supposed to stay and that was that. I had to stand up for myself this time.

The next morning, my roommate left early for class. I woke the man up and I asked him to leave. He said he had nowhere to go. I told him I didn't care, that I never wanted to see or talk to him again. That whatever this was, was over. There were no tears this time. No shouting. No threats. He didn't try to touch me or kiss me. He just looked sad and maybe a little scared. I'd like to think he could see how much he had hurt me, how much he had taken from me, how strong I was trying to be and how angry I was. He finally left. It was over.

I have never seen him again, though every time I go home to visit my family I am scared I will see him. It's been twenty years and I am still scared that I will run into him. It seems silly to admit, but it's true. I hear he has children now. I just don't know what I would even say to him. Actually, that's not true. I do know. I would ask him, "*Why? Why did you do that? Why didn't you let me go?*" I wonder what he would say.

If you happen to be reading this as an adult and have a story like mine in your past, let me say, I'm sorry for our shared experience. If you are reading this as a younger person who's in a similar situation right now, I want to tell you something: No matter how messy the situation seems, how overwhelming it might feel, you can always stop something that you don't want to continue. It's your body and your life and if something feels wrong, it probably is. There are people out there who can help you, there are allies nearby who will support you. You are not trapped. There is always an exit. I wish I'd known that then.

It's Never the Priest You
Want to Kiss

I WOULD LIKE TO CLARIFY THAT MY PREDICAMENT with the forty-year-old did not stem solely from my involvement in the community theater. I must also acknowledge the contributions of the Catholic Church and its complicated path toward manhood.

There are certain benchmarks in the Catholic Church that mark the passing of time as a kid: the Sacraments. Reconciliation, First Communion, and Confirmation are all a Holy Paper Trail tracking your journey to adulthood. At Our Lady of Lourdes, you made your Reconciliation in second grade and your First Communion in third grade, but it was Confirmation, in eighth grade, that everyone looked forward to. That's when you became an adult in the church and you got to pick a symbolic name to represent your new position. (Not that anyone ever called you by this name or you would ever use it in any capacity.) I chose Saint Lawrence the Martyr. He was grilled alive on a spit. Very dramatic.

Beyond the Sacraments, there is also an additional rite of passage for Catholic boys that not everyone is invited to partake in. You have to be *chosen*. It is the time-honored and, in my mind, coveted tradition of becoming an altar boy. My brother Dan was one, so I was familiar with some of the routine and I had already imagined how exciting and, dare I say, *glamorous* the position could be. Coincidentally, I reached altar boy age just as I was also becoming interested in local theater. Weeks after my devastating *Oliver!* audition I was pulled aside at school by Sister Idalia, the nun in charge of training the altar boys, who asked me to join her little army. True, it was not as cool as playing a dirty Dickensian orphan, but it felt good to be picked for something. I was in! Catholic mass seemed to be sort of similar to theater. There were lights, music, singing, costumes, special effects, drama, a big magic show at the end, and then more singing to close it out. I just had to deal with Sister Idalia to get there.

Sister Idalia had been my first grade teacher, and she was a tricky lady. She looked like Mrs. Claus, but she acted more like Miss Hannigan, and I'm still scarred by some of my interactions with her. One time on the playground, I noticed a girl in my class standing all alone with her knockoff Cabbage Patch doll. She had brought it for show-and-tell, which obviously had not gone as planned. She hadn't known that her doll was a knockoff, but she did now and the other girls were making fun of her for it. I felt bad for her, so to try and cheer her up, I took her off-brand doll, and I started doing hopscotch with it. It worked. She started laughing and I felt like I had done something good for another human.

Then Sister Idalia came over to me and said, "Andy, why are you playing like a girl? Boys don't play hopscotch and they definitely DON'T play with dolls!" Then she laughed like the Wicked Witch of the West. God, I hated her for that. I wanted to scream at her, "You think I want to play hopscotch with this piece of shit doll? I'm just trying to make this girl feel better, you old bat!" But I didn't say that to Sister Idalia. Instead I ran to the other side of the playground and left that sad little girl all alone with her sad little doll.

I hadn't spent much time with Sister Idalia since then, but I thought she might treat me differently now that I was an "older" kid. She didn't. She was still a nightmare. But she was less of one, because I was trying very hard to nail this altar boy gig. Also, at this point in my Catholic school career, I had figured out how to slip in my secret weapon: I had four great-aunts who were full-blown nuns. None of them lived in Omaha and two of them were dead, so I didn't know them that well, but I had figured out how to drop that fun fact into religion classes and passing conversations with the nuns at my school. "My aunt has a habit just like yours!" I'd say, or "One of my aunts—WHO'S A NUN—taught me all about virgin births!"

Truth be told, the only insight that my Sister aunts offered me was how unfairly they were treated by the church and how depressing their lives could be. I had heard my grandmother talk about how some of her Sister sisters were given electroshock therapy in the late 1960s for depression when they went through menopause. Living in basic poverty, working tirelessly seven days a week, promising yourself to a man who never came . . . it didn't seem like a lot of fun. I wasn't really factoring all of this information into my feelings for Sister Idalia at this point, but I think it did make me a little more sensitive to her mood swings. And like I said, I was trying VERY hard to be good. I was a total kiss-ass and it was working.

Once we learned all the choreography for the mass, we

would rehearse it over and over again. Sister Idalia would play the priest, and we would take turns practicing the different altar boy positions. If you were on the right, your show was very different from the kid's on the left. Each side had its own important jobs, but in my mind, the right side was more important. It did most of the vital chores when it came to the big magic trick at the end. You got to hand the hosts and wine over to the priest before he turned them into flesh and blood. I remember wondering if I was going to get to see them really transform since I would be standing so close. I would later be disappointed to see there was no physical change whatsoever. Although, I don't know what I would have done if something had actually happened. Sure, the idea of eating flesh and drinking blood is fun in *theory* . . . but if push comes to shove, I think that's a big "No, thank you."

Sister Idalia was a stern taskmaster during rehearsals. She was like the Jerome Robbins of Our Lady of Lourdes Church. She would make us practice the mass until we were perfect. She knew every word by heart, and she took her role of playing the priest very seriously. Looking back now, I think it must have been hard for her to only get to run the show at altar boy practice. She was good at it. She was reverent and dramatic when she needed to be. She was thoughtful and graceful. I'll bet she would have given a good homily, too. She was like the stage manager who dreamed of being the star but who would never be given the chance. It was another reason to feel sad for these ladies: They were never given the responsibilities they so clearly would have excelled at.

One of the final steps of altar boy practice was adding in the costume—I mean, the cassock. It was probably what I was most excited about. The cassocks were white and long, and they had a hood that hung dramatically off the back. Sister Idalia told us we were never, NEVER to put the hoods on. Now I realize that it was because we would have looked like members of the KKK, but I didn't know what that was in the fourth grade, so I just assumed it was because of something mysteriously religious. The accessories for this outfit were a simple wooden cross and a sash that came in all sorts of colors corresponding with the different holy days. Red was my favorite; that was for feast days of martyrs. I think it appealed to me on two levels: I've always loved a martyr story—please see above about Saint Lawrence the Martyr—and I love a classic pop of color. I was dramatic and stylish even as a fourth grader.

I remember putting it all on for the first time and looking in the mirror. I loved my Catholic mass costume. I felt so official and so important. It gave me an identity and a purpose, particularly since I would not be appearing at the Emmy Gifford Theater in the foreseeable future. This Catholic mass stage would have to do for now. Altar boy rehearsals only lasted a couple weeks, and then we were handed over to the priests to perform real mass for a packed church. We had a week of previews first though. We would *serve*—that's what they call it—Monday through Friday at 6:45 a.m. mass, and then, if all went well, we would take on the Saturday show at 5:30 p.m.

Sister Idalia made it clear that the most important job of the altar boy was to support the needs of his priest. They all had slightly different styles, and we had to adjust to each one accordingly. We understood and observed each priest carefully, trying to figure out how we could be his perfect servant. (It wasn't until many years, multiple therapists, and some serious journaling later, that I realized that Sister Idalia was responsible for two very different but very important, and occasionally self-destructive, drives that would shape my adult life: an ambitious need for a career in show business and the feeling that you have to *serve* older men who are in a position of power in your life. Thanks, Sister.)

While Sister Idalia had successfully briefed us on the different priests' needs, what she hadn't prepared us for were their different *personalities*. I quickly learned that Father Russ was kind and patient. Father Tom was rough and his hands shook. Father Rodney was cold and wouldn't look you in the eye. Father Russ was my favorite because he was so nice, but I wanted to impress Father Tom the most. He was the most withholding, so naturally I needed him to like me and say it often. (I'm still unpacking that one with the help of *Oprah's Master Class*.) Father Tom was also the most handsome. He was tall and fit and he had silver hair. Not gray. *Silver.* He usually looked sunburned. I now know that flush was from alcohol, but it still suited him. He was probably in his early fifties and he seemed so manly to me. So authoritative. My mother had a name for priests like Father Tom. She called them "Father What a Waste"s. They were too attractive to be priests, to be celibate. I grew up with this phrase as a useful way to categorize priests at school. If we got a new priest, my mother would ask, "Is he a Father What a Waste?" I got very good at deciding which ones were.

I managed to make it through my first week as an altar boy without any incident. I did everything almost perfectly. Sister

Idalia even said so. So did Father Tom. He patted me hard on the back. I felt good about my first week in his service.

I continued to have my crush on Father Tom, although at that age that's not what I would have called it, and he continued to usually ignore me. It was fine though; I grew to appreciate and romanticize the distance, a pattern that would only become more ingrained in my heart and mind as I grew older. Annoyingly, Father Rodney was the one who always wanted to talk. He always wanted to ask questions about school and teachers and what sports we played. I never liked serving with him. He often seemed sweaty and nervous during mass, and he was always looking over your head or to the side, never right in your eyes. But after mass, it was all chitchat and awkward jokes. I always felt trapped.

Don't worry, this story is not headed where you think it might be headed (at least not yet). Father Rodney never touched me. As weird as he was, he never physically abused anyone to my knowledge. He just had the misfortune of seeming like a creep. That only made my affection for the stern and stoic Father Tom grow even stronger.

From fourth through eighth grade I served those priests well. I was a real Altar Star at Our Lady of Lourdes! But as my Catholic star rose, so did my place on the secular community theater stage, and I was more than happy to trade Christ for lines and better costumes. It was way more fun. My retirement from the altar came just as my interest in it disappeared, but my relationship to priests was just about to kick into high gear.

While my grade school had been run by nuns, my high school, Creighton Prep, was run by priests, Jesuit priests.

Widely considered to be the "cool kids" of the Catholic Church, the Jesuits taught you to question the Church, to rebel at times. To think critically about the teachings of the Church. Some of these priests had been married in the past, some admitted to having sex (only with women), some talked about drinking and smoking. They just seemed . . . cool. And as my mother pointed out, there were several "Father What a Waste"s there.

Freshman year I met another Father Tom. This one was much younger, probably in his early twenties, and very handsome. He taught my Freshman Theology class with a contagious amount of enthusiasm for the Church. He pushed us all to ask questions and wasn't afraid to tell us if he had the same questions. He took note of me early on, and saw that while I might look confident, I wasn't. The first few weeks at Creighton Prep I often ate lunch by myself or sometimes in the bathroom, which now seems insanely unsanitary, but it was better than being seen eating alone.

Father Tom figured this out and asked me if I wanted to eat lunch with him in his office. I agreed, and I found that he had assembled a small group of other awkward freshmen who had also been eating alone. We eventually got to know one another and formed a little group of our own. Father Tom suggested at some point that we all venture out into the lunchroom together. We did and it worked. He had fully assimilated us into the general population. I was grateful to him for that. Afterward, I still visited Father Tom's office from time to time, even after he was no longer my teacher. I had developed a strong crush on him. (At this age, I was fairly certain that's exactly what I'd have called it.) I would often hover in his office, my sexual frustrations spilling out all over the place. I must have reeked of hormonal tension and vulnerability. To his credit, Father Tom never acknowledged my desperation, but other priests did.

Father Don was mostly retired. Old and doughy, he would totter through the halls, talking to young men about classes and sports, usually ending the conversation with a smack on the ass. He used to find me in study hall. He would bend down close to my face and whisper questions in my ear with one hand firmly planted on either my knee or my shoulder. Usually my knee. Sometimes he would just appear behind me and rub my shoulders while talking to me. He started to get bolder as the months went by and would sloppily kiss my cheek when he greeted me, always getting closer and closer to my mouth. This was around the time that I misplaced my virginity with the forty-year-old. I think Father Don sensed that.

And then there was the most disappointing priest of all— I'll call him Father Dominic. He was probably in his sixties, but he worked out every day and remained lean and sinewy. He also took an interest in me because I did well in his classes. That's what I thought anyway. When things really started to get complicated with the forty-year-old, I was at a total loss for adult connection and assistance. My grades were plummeting, I constantly had a stomachache, and I thought my life was crumbling around me. Having no one to talk to about my terrible relationship and feeling hopeless, I decided I would confess to Father Dominic at the next mass. He seemed so strong, but so kind, and I was hopeful that he could save me from myself.

We were made to go to mass once a week, but mass was sort of a hippie affair. It was held in our indoor quad, which was modern for the nineties, and they would start by dimming the lights. We would all sit on the floor, and it all felt very earthy and Jesus-y. Priests mostly didn't wear robes; they just wore their casual, Daytime Priest looks, and we would listen to Toad the Wet Sprocket songs instead of singing traditional church music. It was pretty rad, but at this reconciliation mass, my surging anxiety just wouldn't let me enjoy "I Will Not Take These Things for Granted" for the hundredth time.

Confessions were heard at the end. Again, this was not your typical confession with private rooms and curtains drawn. Priests would set up two chairs close to each other in various darkened corners of the quad, turn on music at a low volume to muddle the sound of confessions, and then you would basically just get right up in a priest's face and whisper your sins. Sometimes he would close his eyes and grab the back of your neck firmly while you confessed. It seemed very "Roman Wrestler" at the time, but looking back it was also very "Abusive Pimp." I waited in line to talk with Father Dominic, who was popular for confessions. I told myself that he was going to be helpful, that this was my best option.

I sat across from him in a dark corner, our knees touching. He grabbed my neck, as expected, and I started to talk. I started to try to explain what was happening with me, but I couldn't make the words come out right. Instead, I started to cry. I was so embarrassed. Father Dominic squeezed my neck harder, and he grabbed both my hands with his free hand. His hands were like baseball mitts. We just sat there while I cried. He finally said, "It's okay. You've done nothing wrong." It wasn't exactly what I was looking for, but it still felt nice. He stood up and pulled me up with him. He hugged me tightly. I felt safe and heard and understood. Then, with unexpected force, he kissed me. On the lips. He muscled his tongue into my mouth and held the back of my head still. Then he released me and made the sign of the cross on my forehead. He smiled.

I walked away, stunned. How could he do that? Right in the open. In a daze I walked through the quad. No one had seen it. How was that possible? I mostly tried to avoid Father Dominic for the rest of the year, but when my mother suggested we invite him, along with some of my teachers, to my graduation party, I didn't have the courage to say, "No, he's a real fucking creep." I had too many other problems at the time. So instead I said, "Great idea, Mom." (I did successfully leave out Father Don. Since he was mostly retired, my parents didn't really know him. I was spared a back rub, so that was a minor win.)

When the happy graduation day rolled around, Father Dominic and some other priests, including both Father Toms, celebrated my graduation with my family at a backyard barbecue. The forty-year-old was also there. (It was a real emotional minefield.) At some point, Father Dominic needed to leave, and he asked if I could show him out. I knew what was coming, but at this point, I didn't care. I had performed and received numerous sex acts with a man I didn't care about, and I just walked around feeling damaged. So what did I care if one more creepy man wanted to kiss me? What did it matter? We stood at my parents' front door and said our good-byes for the final time, and then he grabbed me by the back of the neck and forced his tongue in my mouth. I just stood there and let him. I didn't kiss back, but I also didn't move. He smiled at me and walked to his car. I went into our kitchen and slammed a glass of wine before going back out to the party.

Shortly after, the two Father Toms left, and each gave me a congratulatory handshake. Firmly, fatherly, without an ounce of sexuality or menace. In other words, AN APPRO-PRIATE GOOD-BYE FOR A GRADUATION PARTY. I was able to get the forty-year-old to leave without incident by promising to see him later. He still managed to steal a quick kiss and a grope on his way out. Again, I just let it happen.

Cleaning up after the party, I felt a little numb. I thought, How many teenage boys have to deal with this shit at their graduation parties? Am I the only one? Or was Father Domi-nic just taking a tour of homes and forcing French kisses on young men throughout the city? If I *had* to kiss a priest at my graduation party, why couldn't it have been a priest I *wanted* to kiss? More important, why did I *have* to kiss anyone?

It was time to leave. It was time to leave high school, it was time to leave the Catholic Church, it was time to leave Omaha, and it was time to leave this idea that I had to go along with whatever older man was calling the shots, behind. I was eighteen years old, and I couldn't be anybody's altar boy anymore.

Boy Stuff

P RIESTS! FORTY-YEAR-OLDS! SEXUAL AWAKENINGS!
Oh my! We've covered so much ground already. If it isn't
already clear to you, men have always been a source of confusion for me.

It will not shock you to learn that I grew up mostly surrounded by women. I had three sisters and a mother who
were usually stuck with me while my dad and brother were
off doing "Boy Stuff." My dad always said that I was too little
to go with them on these manly outings, usually fishing trips
or baseball games or runs to the sporting goods store. The
problem was that, eventually, after years of being the "little
kid," I wasn't so little anymore, but now I had zero interest in
spending time with my dad. I'm not sure if my dad excluded
me because he knew, subconsciously, that I was gay, but I
have to be honest—I didn't care. I always preferred hanging
out with the girls. I didn't want to go fishing, I wanted to go
to the mall. I didn't care about baseball games, I cared about
seeing *Overboard* starring Goldie Hawn and Kurt Russell.
My dad and I were just continuing the tradition of straight
fathers keeping a safe distance from their gay sons. We certainly didn't invent the dynamic, we just embraced it.

The only downside it had was that I was inherently uncomfortable around other boys. I didn't speak their language. I would get nervous that they might ask me to catch or kick a sports ball or ask me a question about a WWF wrestler that I had never heard of. I avoided most other little boys my age for fear of being found out, like I was some kind of gender fraud. But then in the first grade I met Joe. He was in my class and pretty quiet. I'm not sure how our first interaction went down, but I'm sure it was when we were both hiding from the other boys aggressively playing Red Rover on our concrete playground. All of a sudden Joe was making me laugh. Then I was making him laugh. And from that day on, it was Andy and Joe all the time.

Obviously in the first grade we were not aware of, nor could we have verbalized, exactly what made us different from other boys, but there was just an unspoken understanding that we were going to do our own thing. Joe introduced me to the magic and wonder of a special lady named—Cher. There were lip-sync contests in his basement to "Gypsies, Tramps & Thieves" and "Dark Lady." (This is why stereotypes exist. Because sometimes they are true.) We also saw movies together at the local dollar movie theater. I remember watching *Joe Versus the Volcano* with him and then fighting about who got to be Meg Ryan when we reenacted it afterward. We also memorized the entire Judy Tenuta comedy album and would take turns reciting it. In short, Joe and I just *got* each other, for several years.

Then puberty kicked in and feelings got complicated. "Gay" started being a thing that we knew about. "Fag" was a name that we would often be called while together, or apart. We realized that we were different from the other boys, and our different*ness* while together made us look even more that way. So we broke up, more or less. I guess that was the first breakup I went through. We went to different high schools and just cut it off.

It seems odd now. There wasn't a fight or a conversation; we just stopped speaking to each other after years of speaking daily. Days of silence became weeks, weeks became months, and then too much time had passed. It would have felt too weird to call him. (I still regret not calling him.)

As I got ready for high school, I figured that I was going to have to change the way I made friends with other guys. I quickly realized that knowing all the words to "Half-Breed" or being able to list the entire original cast of *Into the Woods* was not a bonus. Even though in my mind I wasn't calling myself "gay," I was aware that other people most definitely might call me "gay" out loud. I needed a new strategy. Fortunately, my brother Dan was a senior when I was a freshman and provided me with a strong buffer at first. He had a group of rowdy friends who all worked out in the gym after school. Since he was my ride home, I had to work out after school, too. It terrified me on two levels:

1. Being surrounded by sweaty guys working out might mean I would have to talk to them about "guy stuff."
2. Being surrounded by sweaty guys working out might mean I would get a boner.

Luckily, in that gym, conversations were kept to a minimum and I was able to keep my eyes down and my mind on lifting weights. I was strong, so I could keep up with the other guys, which impressed them, and I wanted that approval. Especially from my brother. I was grateful to Dan for giving me what seemed at the time like a necessary safety net. I became "Little Rannells" to my brother's "Rannells." It was the closest we had ever been.

If the gym was where I started to get other guys to accept me, it was the school dances where I sealed the deal. I was a good dancer by mid-nineties standards, meaning I could *grind*. (I watched Eric Nies religiously, and I still have a soft spot in my heart for the song "Pony" by Ginuwine.) That's when I started to get a reputation for being a ladies' man. It made me uncomfortable because it was a lie, but it also made things easier for me at school. I don't know why my classmates thought I was having sex with these girls, but somehow that became the rumor. I could tell it pleased my brother. I'm sure he was nervous for me walking into the testosterone-fueled zoo that was our high school, but now his little brother had the reputation of being a real slut. Lucky him and me!

The next year at school, my first without the protection and guidance of my brother, I started to find my own way. There were other guys there who were similar to me, not gay necessarily, but who had already decided that the world was much larger than Creighton Prep. I started hanging out with these guys and began to feel more comfortable at school and with myself. These guys thought I was smart and funny, and they didn't care whether or not I was fingering a girl from Marian High School after homecoming. I started making real friends, including one who would be both a savior to me and a constant tormentor. His name was Colin.

Colin.

To this day, the first name I associate with the word "handsome." This Colin, MY Colin, looked like he had walked straight out of a Jane Austen novel. He was tall, with kind eyes, dark curly hair, and a jaw that could cut glass. He floated above everyone at that school. Not like he thought he was better than everyone, but like he was so confident that nothing fazed him at all. He was always cheerful, easygoing, warm. He never had teen acne or bad hair. He was just . . . perfect.

I had long admired him from afar but never had the balls to actually speak to him. Even though these were my years as Omaha's top teen model, I regularly felt like Sloth from *The Goonies* if I was anywhere near Colin. Striking up a conversation with him seemed impossible. But one day, HE approached ME. He had seen my picture in the *Omaha World Herald* LIVING! section, promoting a local dinner theater production of *West Side Story*. He said he thought that it was "cool" that I was doing that. Meaning that *I* was cool. *Cool, Daddy-O.* (I practically did a high kick!) Was this a dream? Was I dying? Amazingly, I kept my composure and managed to have a full conversation with Colin. I don't remember the details because I was too busy marveling at the fact that he didn't have pores and his teeth were perfect. His father was an orthodontist, but I was certain he had been born with those perfect teeth.

Eventually Colin's handsomeness, while still impressive, didn't hold the same power over me. I was able to talk to him like a human, ask questions, not lose consciousness when he was near. We both liked Jack Kerouac, we both wanted to move far away from Omaha, we both wanted to explore the world. We started going to movies, the mall, lunches off campus. I even sat through an entire baseball game with him. Years went by and we remained close like this. In the back, and usually the front, of my mind, I hoped that maybe something more might be happening. The slightest touch, a look that went on too long, might mean something deeper was at play. But I certainly wasn't going to make the first move. It was too dangerous.

Our friendship had begun while I was in the throes of my relationship with the forty-year-old. I was sexually curious, frustrated with my lack of romance, and terribly impatient. I was also too scared to talk to Colin about these feelings I was having for him, so sleeping with a forty-year-old seemed like a safer bet. I assumed the forty-year-old wasn't going to tell anyone. (How incredibly wrong I was, as we have learned.) After my brief but doomed love affair with the dancer, Craig, in Miami, I was more convinced than ever that a painful and regrettable relationship with that older man was all I deserved. Colin was too good for me.

The night of my senior prom I went with my friend Randi, a girl I had done countless community theater shows with. She was beautiful, knew that I was gay, and didn't care in the slightest. She was the perfect teenage beard. Once we arrived, I sought out Colin. He looked more handsome than I had ever seen a man look. We were standing on the edge of the dance floor. "Nightswimming" by R.E.M. was playing. I pretended that Colin was my date and that we were dancing together at our senior prom. He looked so beautiful, I just wanted to be close to him. I tried to step as close to him as I could without being caught. It was nice to pretend for a moment that it was real.

Colin and I graduated from Creighton Prep in May of 1997. That fall he was going to college in Boston and I was going to college in New York. I had dreams of us visiting each other on weekends, continuing our friendship on the East Coast. And who knew? Maybe it would finally grow into something else once we were out of Omaha. I was nothing if not persistent in my daydreams. Toward the end of the summer, days before we were both leaving for college, I decided that it was time for me to tell Colin I was gay. It's embarrassing to admit, but I thought that maybe saying the words to him might spark a shift in our relationship. That if I said it first, now free from the eyes and ears and judgments of high school, then maybe he would say it back to me. I pictured us kissing for the first time on his front porch—in my mind it was raining—with all the passion of Winona Ryder kissing Jake Ryan in *Mermaids*. (I know that's not the actor's name, but that's who he is to me.)

I went to Colin's house, we talked about college and moving details for a while, and then I slowly made my way outside to his front porch so we could say good-bye. The sprinklers were on. It wasn't rain, but it was good enough, and I took it as a sign I should go ahead with my coming-out speech. So . . . I told him. I told him that I was gay and that I really valued his friendship and wanted him to know. Colin smiled and then he hugged me. But it wasn't romantic, it was supportive and loving and what I had been missing for a long time. He told me that he was touched that I told him, that he was proud of me for being honest, and that he loved me and would always be my friend. We said our good-byes and vowed to talk soon, and then I got in my car, drove around the corner, and cried. Yes, there was a part of me that wanted

Colin to love me the way I loved him. Yes, there was a part of me that wished I were in his bed at that moment instead of alone in my Ford Escort listening to "Kissing You" by Des'ree. But I realized what was more important, more than any romance, was that he was my friend, and had been for years. Colin was the first non-theater friend I had said those words, *I am gay*, to, and I had been met with love and support. I fell in love with him more deeply that night, but not how I'd expected. (Side note: We are still friends today.)

Days later Colin and I both left Nebraska. No offense to the Omaha school system, but I had very little clue about how close Boston and New York actually were to each other. Had I known it was just a few hours away on the Fung Wah Bus, I probably would have visited Colin immediately. But I didn't know that, and what's more I was preoccupied with making my place in New York. Still, I had a Colin-sized hole in my heart, and I was afraid that nothing would repair it.

Then I met Chris the second month of college. He was sitting on the floor outside of the drama department offices reading *Sam Shepard: Seven Plays*. Gorgeous, dangerously thin, with blue-gray eyes and floppy hair, he *was* Jordan Catalano. He said hello to me and my heart stopped. We had a very casual, not flirtatious conversation, and it quickly became clear to me that he was not gay. Even without the potential of romance, I enjoyed talking to him, and slowly my disappointment switched to hopefulness that I was making a new friend. Maybe he could be my Colin in New York. He seemed friendly and it didn't hurt that he was beautiful. We exchanged numbers and agreed that we would "hang out" sometime. Just like that, I had my first straight, male, college friend.

It took us a couple weeks to actually hang out, and when we did, Chris suggested we go to an Irish pub in the West Village called Fiddlesticks. As I type that line, I am reminded how confused I was by this suggestion. In 1997, the West Village was still über gay. But an Irish pub in the West Village? Not so gay. I figured maybe it was his effort to split the difference for us. Even though we were both underage, we were served copious amounts of alcohol that night. I began to understand why Chris had picked this bar. We were laughing and joking, and I quickly found that I really liked him. I was able to be myself with him, and he seemed totally relaxed with me. Then . . . he kissed me. He kissed me hard. In an Irish pub in the West Village. It was like all the romance of *Titanic* and Baz Luhrmann's *Romeo + Juliet* wrapped up into one teenage kiss. (Basically it was like I was kissing Leonardo DiCaprio.) The kissing quickly grew too explicit for our surroundings and Chris invited me to his apartment. I forgot to mention that he lived in an APARTMENT, not a DORM. Big difference. I said "Yes," probably too quickly, and before I knew it I was having sex with my new "I assumed he was straight" friend.

We started dating. Like, cute nineteen-year-old dating. Cheap dinners, discount theater tickets, free outdoor concerts. We were having lots of enthusiastic sex all over the place—my dorm, his apartment, backstage at the theater in our college, one time in the teachers' lounge after hours. In short, I was being a reckless teen and it felt great. And right under the wire. (At nineteen, I was cutting it close.) While there were times that I missed having a boy *friend* in Chris, I convinced myself that it was better to have a *boyfriend*. And after all, isn't that what I'd learned from my friendship with

Colin? Recent history had shown me you can't have a friend in a lover, you get one or the other. That was apparently how relationships work.

Alas, my teenage love affair with Chris only lasted as long as the school year. As it turns out, Chris wasn't really gay, or at least not gay enough. After we split, he started dating girls and last time I checked—thanks, Facebook—he was married to a woman. He was a bit of a liberal arts college unicorn in those days before we talked about "sexual fluidity": the straight man willing to give homosexuality a try, at least for a semester. Still, I was happy to explore with Chris, and I hope he got as much out of it as I did. I loved him with my whole nineteen-year-old heart. I still have fond memories of making out with him to Sarah McLachlan's *Fumbling Towards Ecstasy*. I have to fight an erection anytime I hear "Hold On."

I was feeling as confused as ever about my relationships with men. With Colin I had the friendship but not the sex. With Chris I had the sex but no longer the friendship. Exhausted by trying to figure these boys out, I decided a better use of my time would be to focus on why I came here in the first place. I would make New York City my boyfriend instead.

One night, some of my fellow Marymount classmates thought it would be fun to try and crash the MTV Music Awards after-party. How they knew where it was, I have no clue, but I tagged along. Of course no one was going to let us into that party, so we ended up just standing in line hoping to see famous people. Then an older man, probably well into his sixties, got out of a car and was being ushered into the party. He saw me in line and smiled. I smiled back. He whispered something to the doorman, and the doorman walked over to me and said, "How many are in your group?"

I panicked. "Ummm . . . four," I replied, even though I was with about nine people.

"Grab your friends," the doorman said.

I turned around and said to no one in particular, "Let's go!" (I figured they could sort out who was coming in with me *Lord of the Flies*–style.)

The doorman let us in, and I was shocked and thrilled. How was this possible? Who was that man? He was waiting for me inside the party. He introduced himself and explained that he was a music producer. He asked if I was a singer. I told him I was studying acting and that I had just moved from Nebraska. His face lit up as if I had said, "I'm a dumb hick with no moral boundaries!" He gave me his business card and told me to call him in the morning. "Have fun with your friends tonight." He shook my hand and that was it. He seemed professional and straightforward.

I called him the next day and we chatted on the phone. I thanked him for getting me into the party. He asked me about classes and how I liked New York. It was, once again, a pretty uneventful conversation. He said, "I get invited to a lot of fun events. Maybe you would want to join me sometime."

"That sounds great!" I said. He told me he would be in touch. He called about a week later to invite me to a party. There was a dinner beforehand, and a whole group of people would be there. A group sounded safe to me.

"Wear a suit" was his only suggestion.

I was naive but not totally stupid. I knew there was a big chance that he wanted something else from me. But I also thought that I was smarter than that. That I could handle it if he tried to make a move. I felt the adventure was worth the risk.

I met the man and his friends at a restaurant on the Upper East Side. Everyone was very nice and made me feel welcome. They never made me feel like a dumb kid, or like someone to be looked down on. We went to the party, I had a good time, and then I went home. Nothing shady. This continued for months. He would invite me to a party with his friends, I would go, and nothing would happen. He was nice and seemed interested in me. He gave me little pieces of advice about the business or meeting people. We were never alone, and I never felt like he put me in an awkward position. My friends were always a little skeptical when I would meet him, but I was too clueless to care. "It's like a work thing," I would explain to them.

"Just be careful," they warned. I refused to accept that there was anything to be careful about. *This wasn't a gross old man. He likes me for me. I'm making better choices.*

One day he called and asked me to dinner. "I want to take you to Shun Lee," he said. "Have you ever had shark fin soup?" The thought of it sounded disgusting, but I cheerfully agreed to go. I walked into Shun Lee, which was the fanciest restaurant I had ever stepped foot in, expecting a group. There was no group this time. It was just the two of us. I was immediately uneasy. Something felt different.

I was correct. Something was different. He said to me that night, "Do you like going to these parties with me? Do you like meeting my friends?"

"Of course," I said, already scared of where this conversation was going.

"That's good to hear. I like you coming with me, Andrew. Do you think you could show me how much you like spending time with me and my friends?"

I felt so stupid for thinking I was smart, that I had figured him out. Of course this is what he wanted. Why would he have taken an interest in me? I was nobody, I had nothing to add, nothing to offer. Well, nothing to offer except what he had wanted all along.

"I don't think I can do that," I said.

He stared at me for a long time. Then he said, "I'm sorry to hear that."

We finished our dinner—the shark fin soup was as disgusting as it sounds—and he asked for the check. We stepped outside, where he had a car waiting for him.

"Are you sure about this?" he asked.

I paused for longer than I needed to. I guess I didn't want to hurt his feelings. That seems so silly now. He was the one who had hurt mine.

"Yes, I'm sure."

With that, he shook my hand and said, "Good luck, Andrew."

That was the last time I heard from him or saw him.

Lesson learned: If it walks like a duck and talks like a duck and the duck is an older, rich guy, he's going to try and fuck you eventually.

I'm nearly twenty years old, I thought. *Shouldn't I have everything figured out by now?* I thought that being a man who dated men would give me some extra insight as to how all of this should work. But instead it was proving to be just as complicated as *When Harry Met Sally* made straight relationships seem. And I thought my new gay insight had mentally and emotionally taught me how to protect myself from dirty old men, but here I was feeling like Tootie in *Facts of Life* when she tried to be a model for that one episode. But wait . . . why did I think that being a gay man would help me relate to other men?

I was having a Bobby in *Company* moment.

C'mon! You're onto something, Bobby. You're onto something!

Maybe men are hard to understand, whether or not you got asked to do the "Boy Stuff" growing up. And maybe, just maybe, people are just really complicated and you can never plan on them doing anything that you expect them to do. Or even more, what you hope they will do.

I can't tell you that this realization was comforting exactly, but it did calm me a bit. If my relationship with my father and brother was any indication, it just took me a little bit longer to find my common ground with other men. What's more, I didn't need a boyfriend at this very second. I had things to focus on: school, a budding career, friendships. And if friendships with women were easier for me to navigate, who cares? What's wrong with that? Maybe that's just where I was at the moment, maybe that's where I would be for a while, and that was okay with me. I felt certain a boyfriend would arrive at some point.

In the meantime, there was fun to be had. And I had the perfect person to have it with.

Taking Requests

THIS IS THE STORY OF TWO PEOPLE WHO MET AND almost instantly became best friends. It's also the story of seeing yourself in someone else for the first time and realizing, "Hey. That person is a lot like me. And if they exist and they act and think similarly to me, that must mean that I am not a mistake and maybe, just maybe, there are even more people out there like *us*."

Zuzanna and I met while auditioning for college scholarship money at the National Foundation for Advancement in the Arts event in Miami. (Years later the organization wisely changed their name to the much catchier YoungArts. It is, to this day, a wonderful resource, and I highly recommend that high school students interested in studying the arts look into it.) I was coming from Omaha, Nebraska; she was coming from Fort Wayne, Indiana. They were two very different cities, but in the eyes of many of the students there from the East and West Coasts, they might as well have been the same place. These kids instantly assumed that we were "farm kids." We were not.

Or even better, they would say, "Oh! You're from a *flyover* state!" They loved that one. People still love that one. As if nothing between the East and West Coasts matters. Being from the middle of the country immediately puts you on the defensive. You find yourself exaggerating the number of people who live in your hometown, or saying things like "I've never even SEEN a cow!" or "We have a TON of gang violence in Omaha!" I heard Zuzanna acting out similar scenes with other students when we first got to Miami.

When we were finally introduced, I felt like we could both breathe a sigh of relief because we didn't have to explain ourselves and our homelands. Zuzanna had a serious leg up on me, though. While she had lived in Fort Wayne since she was a toddler, she was born in Warsaw, Poland. (Exotic!) She and her parents were political refugees who had been shut out of Poland when martial law was imposed in 1981. (Very exotic!) She had the same Midwestern apologetic-ness to her that I had, but she also had a Slavic edge that I lacked. What we both had was an aggressive sarcasm and a mild dislike/envy for the students from more cosmopolitan areas. We wanted what they had, but we also hated them for it.

It's not that we thought we were "too cool" for our surroundings. Much to the contrary, I think that although we both felt like we were talented and deserved to be there, we also knew that we were coming at this sideways. Most of these kids were from performing arts schools in big cities. They were loud and intimidating and they all knew one another. They talked about taking the subway to school, having sex, doing drugs. They had agents and had auditioned for TV shows and Broadway plays. It instantly felt like we were behind. Zuzanna and I walked around in a fog of inferiority and apology, with insane ambition and rage bubbling underneath. (This basically sums up a lot of the Midwest, FYI.)

If I knew I liked Zuzanna immediately, I truly bonded with her the second day we were in Miami. We were lining up for lunch behind some dancers who were all, despite the fact that we were on a break, still doing various forms of choreography for each other. Zuzanna looked at them with disdain and said, "Look at them. Just flaunting their *longness*." I had been thinking the same thing. We were both eighteen, wide-eyed, and jaded, all at the same time.

And there was something different about Zuzanna, something that stirred up my need to be liked and valued and praised for my general awesomeness. I was used to girls chasing me at this point, particularly girls in theater. Not in a sexual way, or at least not always, but for friendship. Girls liked me. I think there is something in a theater girl's DNA that has trained her to seek out gay companionship. It's the same force that naturally pulls gay boys toward girls with big personalities and big hair, who sometimes wear character shoes long after rehearsal is over. But Zuzanna was not your typical theater girl. She didn't chase anyone. She made you come to her, which made her even more intriguing.

We had several conversations that first week and learned that we were different from each other in a lot of ways. She was an only child; I came from a big family. She had traveled the world; I had never left the country. She was incredibly smart and applying to only Ivy League schools; I was barely passing my high school classes. But there was so much we had in common. We both loved and despised where we were coming from. We both knew we wanted more out of life than our current friends were expecting for themselves. And we were also both able to be freely excited with each other about the prospects that awaited us in New York. It was exciting to get to talk with someone who was about to do the same thing I was. Someone who didn't think it was "scary" or "brave." That it was just the natural thing to do. The thing we *had* to do.

Zuzanna also bore witness to my brief yet meaningful relationship with Craig, the dancer with whom I had my tumultuous two-day affair in Miami. Zuzanna was rooming with our new friend Celestina, and Craig and I went to pick them up for a party. While the girls finished getting ready, Craig and I were holding hands on their balcony, feeling feelings and falling in something: Love? Like? I turned around and saw Zuzanna and Celestina peeking out of the bathroom, one head on top of the other, a position I had only seen on *Scooby-Doo* and, I believe, *The Beverly Hillbillies*. Their faces were pure joy and acceptance, and I was so touched that we were all exactly where we wanted to be in that moment.

This trip to Miami, away from our families, was just a little glimpse into what our futures would hold. We were on the cusp of adulthood, moments away from being free of our parents and families and whoever we were in high school. Zuzanna was the first person I ever met who fully understood, without explanation, the beauty and seductiveness of reinvention. I told her that when I got to New York, I was no longer going to be "Andy Rannells," I was going to be "Andrew Rannells." *Andy* was an unsure kid who got himself into trouble. *Andrew* was going to be more confident and decisive. She told me that when she was growing up in Fort Wayne, her parents insisted that everyone call her "Susan" instead of "Zuzanna" so that she seemed more American.

When she got to Barnard in the fall, she was going to be "Zuzanna" full-time. She didn't need to pretend she was born here. There was no shame in being an immigrant. We were both emigrating to New York and being set on the path to being who we wanted to truly be—new names, new city, new lives. We were going to find ourselves in New York, damn it. Whether it was ready for us or not. We also decided that she was going to wear darker lipstick and I was going to socially smoke. We had a lot of plans.

Zuzanna and I moved to New York a week apart. I was at Marymount and she was at Barnard. I felt a little embarrassed by my school choice, but I was so proud of Zuzanna and her fancy Ivy League university. I know she was proud of herself, too, but we both wished we were at NYU. We wanted to be in a more prestigious acting program. I couldn't afford it, and her parents had insisted that she get a more well-rounded education. (In the years that would follow, anytime we walked by an NYU building or one of the many purple NYU flags that dotted the city, Zuzanna and I would flip them off. If we couldn't have what we wanted, fuck them. It was a very mature approach.)

The first night we hung out in the city took a lot of coordinating. This was pre–cell phones, kids, so we chatted on our landlines and decided to meet in a location that seemed easy enough to find for two people who had just moved to the city: Union Square. I guess we didn't realize just how large Union Square was. Once I arrived, I was waiting on the west side of the park, while Zuzanna was waiting on the east side. Then I walked to the east while she walked to the west. We did this multiple times, missing each other with each pass. It was like the platonic, teen version of *Sleepless in Se-attle*. I don't know why we both had the same instinct, but at a certain point, we both made our way toward Washington Square Park. Maybe it was the gravitational pull of NYU in our hearts. And there, near the arch, blocks away from where we'd intended to meet, we found each other. It was our version of the top of the Empire State Building, I guess.

At this point, we were nineteen and couldn't really get into any bars, particularly in Greenwich Village, where establishments were used to underage college students trying to talk their way inside. There were several humiliating attempts and the inevitable rejections when we didn't have proper ID. We played so many versions of that scene. Sometimes we would "discover" in front of the bouncer that we had forgotten our IDs. "My ID must be in my other purse!" Or "Wait, I thought YOU said you would carry our IDs. Women! Am I right, man?" Sometimes we would be belligerent. "You're joking, right? I'm twenty-two, sir." Or "I come here all the time! We're friends with the owner!" And sometimes we would just try to walk in with authority and pretend we didn't speak English. Nothing worked.

We wandered all over the Village that night, and then, by some extraordinary stroke of luck, we walked by a tiny bar that had loud piano music pouring out of it. Not just music, but *show tunes*. It was called "Rose's Turn," a charming tribute to the finale of one of the greatest musicals of all time, *Gypsy*. We took it as a sign. Zuzanna had played a Hollywood Blonde in a community theater production in Fort Wayne and I, well, I'm gay and just love *Gypsy*. As we crept in, an older man was singing "Anthem" from *Chess*. The bar was

located in a basement with a low ceiling, even lower lighting, and a smattering of patrons all in or around their fifties.
We took our seats at a small table near the door. A waitress
absentmindedly asked us what we wanted to drink. Success! I
ordered what I considered to be the most sophisticated drink
I could think of, "A Tanqueray and tonic, please." Zuzanna
got a whiskey sour. We tucked in with our drinks and tried
to be invisible.

It didn't last long. The piano player spotted us and asked if
we were going to sing something. I was immediately thrilled
and petrified. *Me? Sing in a New York bar?* I started thinking of songs that I could fire off without much effort. Maybe
the Tanqueray hit me faster than I thought, but my mind
landed on a rather odd choice, especially considering that
I had devoted nearly all of my teen years to obsessing over
musical theater. I walked up to that piano player and said,
"Do you know 'Copacabana' by Barry Manilow?" He looked
a little surprised and then said, "Yes, I do." Before I knew it,
I was belting out "Her name was Lola! She was a showgirl!"
in a West Village bar. Zuzanna's face worked its way through
horror and amazement before finally settling on joy.

I felt a real rush singing that night. I was standing in front
of about ten people total, but they were all listening to me,
watching me perform. And they liked it! It is this rush of fear
mixed with pride that makes performing so addictive, and it
was the first time I had felt it since I had arrived in New York.
Yes, this was a small stage, but in many ways, it was my New
York debut.

After my song, a round of drinks was sent over to us by a
man at the bar. "Great song choice!" he shouted. We waved

a thank-you and guzzled our drinks. The piano player asked if Zuzanna wanted to sing something. She had done several musicals in high school but didn't consider herself to be a singer. She politely declined. Our waitress got up to sing a few songs. She was clearly working through some emotional upheaval, and we were moved by her renditions of "As Long as He Needs Me" and a song we had never heard, "Fifty Percent" from the musical *Ballroom*. There was a lot of angst in that bar. I was starting to see why "Copacabana" had played so well.

After our cocktail waitress's gloomy set, I decided to take another go at it. I requested to sing another classic, "Can't Take My Eyes Off of You." Most people know this song as the huge hit by Frankie Valli. I, however, only knew it as the encore of the *Vikki Carr: Live at the Greek Theatre* album my parents owned. I had no idea anyone else had ever sung it. Needless to say, my rendition was a little different from Frankie Valli's. It just reeked of Vikki and a late-sixties lounge act. More drinks were sent over, and Zuzanna and I continued to consider ourselves extremely lucky that we had found this magical Brigadoon of a bar.

In between songs and chatter, Zuzanna and I drank and laughed and talked about the various anxieties of moving to New York fresh out of high school. Hours passed. In my gin haze I was struck by how comfortable this all was with her. We didn't really know each other well, but sitting together, having this evening, this talk, these laughs, it was just *easy*. I had friends back in Omaha whom I felt a certain kinship with, but none of them were doing what I was doing. None of them had uprooted themselves to take a running leap at a dream they'd had since childhood. Zuzanna was doing it, and she understood why I was doing it, too. We both had big dreams and were prepared to take big swings.

I went to the bathroom while another waitress started to sing "Alone Again (Naturally)." (I'm telling you, the staff should have been on suicide watch.) From the bathroom I heard the song end and the applause that followed. Then I heard silence. A long silence. I wasn't sure what was happening out there. I feared the bar was being held up by robbers or maybe one of the waitresses was finally ending her public breakdown. Then I heard low talking through the microphone. I slowly opened the door to the bathroom, slightly concerned about what I was returning to. I recognized the sound. It was Zuzanna doing her college scholarship audition monologue. It was a very moving, somewhat strange piece from Tony Kushner's *A Bright Room Called Day*. In it a woman is talking about being in a production of *Faust*. She fears that if the devil actually appeared before her to offer her everything she had ever wanted in exchange for her soul, the devil wouldn't bother because she wasn't worth it. It's a wonderful monologue, but looking back it seems both jarring and yet incredibly moving coming from a nineteen-year-old girl. My monologue had been from George Bernard Shaw's *Man and Superman*. I'd never really known what I was talking about when I performed it.

Zuzanna was standing next to that piano in a pink spotlight, fully committed to this performance. The entire bar sat silently watching this young woman completely lose herself in these words. I doubt there had ever been, or would ever be again, a monologue performed at Rose's Turn. She crushed it. The patrons were moved, the waitresses both related to the piece with a little too much enthusiasm, and I was floored by my new friend's talent and confidence. During her well-earned applause, we went back to our table and more free drinks were sent our way. Zuzanna was immediately horrified by what she had done, but I think also proud of the fact that she had won the crowd over with her unexpected performance.

At that age, there was no verbal outpouring of affection for each other. No showering of praise for individuality. We were buzzed on free liquor and the acceptance of strangers. We were hundreds and hundreds of miles away from home and our families, and yet we had started to take the first steps toward making a new life in New York. And even more important, we were falling in love with each other as friends, and with our new chosen home.

Over the next couple years, before we could legally drink, we visited Rose's Turn often. Sometimes we brought friends with us, guys we were dating, guys we wanted to date. But many times it was just Zuzanna and me, laughing and catching up, enabling each other for better or worse.

"Don't go to work tomorrow!"

"You can skip class!"

"You should definitely audition for that part."

"Don't call him back. He's not worth it."

Rose's Turn was not young or hip or sexy; in fact, it was a little busted, but it was friendly and it suited us perfectly. And it gave us a chance to perform, a place to act like we were real actors and not just students. No matter how insecure you were in an acting class, or how demoralizing an audition was, you could always depend on being able to take the stage at Rose's Turn and get a warm "Hello!" and some applause. They always remembered what we drank, but they never asked too many questions. They accepted us as whoever we presented when we walked in the door. If we were two veteran actors who needed a drink to shake off the day, then that's who we were. It was our very own *Cheers,* if *Cheers* had been about a piano bar with older New Yorkers belting Sondheim in it.

We went back to visit our friends at Rose's Turn close to a decade after we had first discovered it. The staff was mostly the same. That first waitress we'd had was still there, and she was singing when we arrived. She greeted us over the microphone and then said to the rest of the bar, "These kids have been coming in since they were too young to drink!" It's silly, but it felt nice to be remembered. Today, Rose's Turn is closed, like so many of the places Zuzanna and I used to visit when we first moved to New York. I feel like maybe one day we will open our own piano bar, catering to newcomers and lost souls in New York. You can sing whatever you'd like, and monologues are more than welcomed.

Summer Stock

(or Things You Can Learn in a Barn)

DURING MY FIRST YEAR IN NEW YORK, EVERY Thursday, without question, I would stop at the newsstand on my way to Marymount and pick up a copy of what I considered to be a sure ticket to getting me the career of my dreams: *Backstage*. *Backstage* is a trade paper that lists every audition happening in the city, whether for Broadway chorus lines, smaller regional theaters, or "student films" that may or may not involve you taking your clothes off. It's a cornucopia of possibility, and I happily paid the two dollars it cost every week to get it.

Honestly, most weeks there was really nothing to get excited about. At nineteen, I was not in the actors union and still in school, so my options were limited. Then, one week, in the spring of my freshman year, I picked up a particularly thick edition of *Backstage*. It felt fuller than usual, like there was more hope inside. I sat alone in the strangely dim cafeteria at Marymount and slowly turned the pages, ready to circle as many auditions as possible with the executive-style red Swiss Army pen my dad had given me as a graduation gift. I used this pen exclusively for journaling and *Backstage* circling. It was meant only for serious business.

There were so many auditions in this issue, and nearly all

of them met my requirements: non-union, summertime only, and in the New York tristate area. I couldn't believe my luck. I started noticing the names of the theaters. Oddly, almost all of them seemed to contain the words "Barn" or "Summer." And how was it possible that each of these theaters would be casting six shows in a three-month period? Then it hit me and I felt like such a fool for not thinking of it sooner; these were SUMMER STOCK theaters.

For those of you who don't know, summer stock is an age-old tradition that young actors have been participating in for generations. You are paid very little to work very hard, all in the name of professional experience and fun, with a potential side of offstage romance and extracurricular drama. There were at least five theaters having auditions that week that included shows I was right for. I started hatching my plan. I couldn't go to every audition, because some were happening on the same day at the same time, and each involved spending the better part of my day lining up and waiting for my turn to sing my sixteen bars of music and hope for the best. (It's worth pointing out here that sixteen bars is about thirty seconds of a song. It is your job as the auditionee to pack as much excitement into those thirty seconds as possible. Translation: Sing as high and loud as you can. It turns out my mother's advice was right once again. Thanks, Charlotte!)

I started comparing the theaters, but I hadn't heard of any of them, so I didn't have much to go off of. I decided I would rank them by the shows they were doing that season and their proximity to New York City. One immediately jumped out at me: the Theater Barn. It was in New Lebanon, New York, located in the "heart of the Berkshires." Wherever that was. Their season included *The Fantasticks, Forever Plaid, The Mousetrap, Grease,* and *Promises, Promises.* I was not familiar with *The Mousetrap* or *Promises, Promises,* but there were definitely roles in those other shows for me, and good ones. I asked one of my acting teachers how close the Berkshires were to the city.

"About three hours. Are you looking for summer stock work? It's great experience. Some of the best training you can get as a young actor."

I was in.

The day of my Theater Barn audition I had to skip class to go. Fortunately, I didn't have any classes I considered important that day—just core classes like Literature and Ecology and a remedial math class. You know? Nothing practical. I showed up at Shetler Studios, which at the time was on Eighth Avenue and 55th Street. It was a rickety building with one terrifying elevator that carried groups of ten nervous young hopefuls up to the eighth floor to have their talent judged and their egos potentially bruised. The hallways were packed with people. The whole space smelled like hairspray and anxiety B.O. covered with CK One. I had never been to an audition like this before. It was a zoo. My *Rent* experience seemed so civilized now. There hadn't been many people there, and they'd been expecting me, welcomed me even. This was like musical *Gladiator.* I had to push my way to the sign-up sheet, which was guarded by a woman sitting behind a folding table with a clipboard and a pen. It was a little after 9 a.m., but she already had a look on her face that said, "I will happily commit domestic terrorism in this audition space if provoked." I nervously told her my name, and she informed me that I would be number 156. *156?!* I thought. *How was that even possible? How early did these people get here? I thought I was on time!*

"How long will that take?" I asked.

She looked at me like she might snap my neck without a second thought.

"After lunch. Maybe sooner. I don't know. Stay close!" she barked back.

I found a little spot on the floor and took a seat. In my backpack I had my audition music and a collection of essays and poems called *The Beat Reader.* (I was very much into Jack Kerouac and his pals at the time. What can I say? At nineteen I was a serious actor, a serious person, and I only read "serious" things. If I'd owned a monocle, I probably would have been wearing it.) What I had not packed was water or a snack. Now, a normal person might figure that since he had 155 people auditioning ahead of him, it was probably safe to run to the corner store for some Poland Springs and a Snickers. But not this kid! Nope! I was certain that the second I left, they would call my name. So I stayed and sat and read, and sat some more and pretended to read some more, eavesdropped on conversations, and waited for my turn. Close to four hours passed. I was parched and dizzy from hunger, but I refused to leave.

Finally a list of names were called, including mine, and we were told to line up. My anxiety kicked into high gear. Even though I'd had nothing to eat or drink for hours, I now had to urinate badly. But there was no time. I stood in line listening to the people ahead of me try and make the most of their brief time in the room. I started to feel like maybe I should flee. I mean, who cares if I just wasted an entire day? I don't need a summer stock job. I could just go to Omaha and get a job there for the summer. I had always wanted to work at the Henry Doorly Zoo as the guide on the zoo train. I would get to point out the giraffes and okapis. Maybe this was my chance. As I was planning my escape, the door to the audition room opened and the mean-looking lady at the folding table, now even meaner-looking, yelled, "Next!"

This was it. I had thirty seconds to let these people know that they should be hiring me immediately. I left the safety of the line and walked into the room. No one spoke to me. There was a group of about ten people all sitting behind a line of tables that were covered with snacks and beverages. My hunger and dehydration hit me like a dodgeball. I thought about asking for a swig of one of their waters, but it seemed inappropriate. I gave the accompanist my music and walked to the center of the room. An older woman who sat in the middle of the group finally addressed me.

"What are you singing?"

" 'Amazing Journey' from *The Who's Tommy*," I announced proudly.

In the sixteen-bar tradition, I had selected the highest and loudest portion of the song to perform. It was pleasantly aggressive at best and obnoxiously showy at worst. I planted my feet and belted out that song with all the power I could muster. Sometimes when an audition goes well, you sort of leave your body for a moment. It's like you can see yourself performing; it's all instinct. That's how I felt when I sang this particular song. It fit perfectly in my voice, and I didn't have to think too hard about it. When an audition goes badly, you also leave your body, but for different reasons. It's like seeing your life flash before your eyes when you are struck by lightning or the moment before you are hit by a train. This was the good type though. I finished the song and walked to the piano to get my music. "Thank you!" I said to no one in particular and started for the door. The whole room laughed.

"Whoa!" the woman at the table said. "Give us just one second."

They all started whispering among themselves. I stood nervously by the door, excited but also wanting to run screaming into the hallway.

"Do you know anything from *The Fantasticks*?" the woman asked.

As it turns out, I had played the role of Matt in *The Fantasticks* my senior year of high school in Omaha, at two different theaters. I loved that show.

"Yes. I know the whole show."

The room laughed again. I didn't feel in on the joke, but I smiled along.

"Can you sing 'I Can See It' for us?"

"I Can See It" is the big second-act number for Matt. It's loud and high and really exciting if it goes well. Had I been thinking clearly I should have said, "No, I don't really know it, but I would be happy to give it a try, I guess." And then belted them into oblivion. But I had already shown my cards.

"Yes, I can," I said.

The accompanist started playing, and I sang with all the power and passion in my nineteen-year-old body. Again I had the experience of being outside myself. There was no time to think about anything, I was just reacting. I was present and honest and suddenly not afraid of anything. Or maybe I was just delusional from hunger. Either way, it was satisfying. The song ended. They were all smiling.

"Thank you, Andrew," the woman said.

I left the room feeling drunk on confidence and ready to collapse at any moment. I walked across the street to a Wendy's and ate a large bacon cheeseburger and downed a bucket of Coke. I felt good and, for the first time in ages, like I had in Omaha. I felt like that job was mine.

Fortunately, it was. That woman from the audition room called me the next day. Her name was Joan Phelps and she owned the Theater Barn. She offered me the entire season, starting with *The Fantasticks*, then *Forever Plaid*, then *Grease*, and ending with *Promises, Promises*. I would rehearse a show for two weeks and then run it for two weeks while rehearsing the next show. I would also be expected to perform certain backstage and front-of-house jobs, such as helping with set building and light cleaning in the lobby between shows. The season was from June to the last week of August, and I would be paid $150 a week plus room and board for the summer. It was a lot of information to take in.

I was thrilled at my win but also concerned about some of the details. "Set building" and "light cleaning"? $150 a week? I hesitated on the phone just long enough for Joan to launch into a speech that she must have given hundreds of times over the years to hundreds of actors like me. She started explaining the value of a season of summer stock, the opportunity to work with great directors and great actors. She even referenced the lack of credits on my résumé and how this season would help me remedy it. It seemed like a low blow, but she was right. My head started to spin. I needed the experience and I needed a job. Period.

I accepted the job and that was that. I had committed to my first summer stock season. I would be singing and dancing all summer in a barn. *C'mon, kids!* I thought. *Let's put on some shows!*

School ended, and I was able to go to Omaha for a couple of weeks before I had to report for duty in the Berkshires. I was now getting nervous about the reality of my summer. I had *just* started to feel settled into New York and my routine there—my commute to school, my nights out with Zuzanna, which old bodega lady would give me free coffee because she thought I was James Van Der Beek—and now I was uprooting myself. I didn't really know where I was going, I wouldn't know anyone once I got there, and I would be living in a house with these strangers for the next three months. But I was going to try to stay positive.

After a quick visit home, during which my mom repeatedly reminded me of how thin I was and how sad she was I couldn't stay home for the summer, I packed my bags and left Omaha once again, this time bound for Albany, where Joan Phelps would pick me up and drive me to the Theater Barn. The day I traveled it was raining and my flight was delayed. When I finally arrived I saw Joan. She looked markedly less friendly than the last time I had seen her. She was wearing an oversized Garth Brooks T-shirt and faux-denim stirrup pants. (Her feet were not in the stirrups, which were just dangling off the back, just to give you a clear visual.) It was obvious Joan was pissed that I was late, and she seemed eager to punish me, as though I had personally flown the plane in the wrong direction just to annoy her.

"We gotta move!" she yelled. "I have a show opening to-night and we can't be late!"

I nervously waited for my luggage while she looked at her watch and aggressively sighed every three seconds. When I finally got my bag, we ran to her eighties Cadillac and she raced out of the parking lot.

"Mind if I smoke?" she said.

"Not at all," I said, and she quickly took out a pack of Merits. We sat mostly in silence for the hour-long ride to the theater. As I stared out the window, I noticed that the Berkshires were actually really pretty. I had never been that far north in New York, and it looked and felt like a different state entirely. It kind of reminded me of western Nebraska but with more trees. And more color. And mountains. Okay, it wasn't that much like Nebraska, but there were cows, at least. I guess that was where the similarities stopped.

I had no idea where I was going, so I was just trusting this stranger to deliver me to this wonderful experience that I had been promised. We finally arrived at the Theater Barn and much to my surprise . . . it was a barn. It wasn't built to look like a barn, nor was it "barn-like," it was just a fucking barn. It hadn't occurred to me that this would be the case.

"There she is," Joan said rather proudly. "I'm going to take you to the house and then you can walk over to the theater to see opening night of *Tintypes*. Your El Gallo just arrived today, too. His name is Steve." (El Gallo is the male lead of *The Fantasticks*, and is usually played by a swarthy baritone. As for *Tintypes*, I didn't know what the hell that was.)

We pulled up to "the house," which was a rather run-down-looking white farmhouse with a screened-in porch and several cars parked on the grass outside. Joan did not show me inside. She just came to a stop and said, "Take one of the bedrooms upstairs. I think there's an empty bed in the back room. You'll have to share with one of the *Tintypes* actors. Don't be late for the show tonight!" With that, she sped her car off the front lawn, leaving a trail of cigarette smoke in her faux-denim wake.

I dragged my suitcase into the house. It was . . . bleak. Dirty and sad, and the furnishings looked more like a last-minute yard sale than a home. I wandered around looking for signs of life. There were bedroom doors open, revealing suitcases exploded onto twin beds. The house had been left as if The Rapture had come and everyone had been saved mid-chore. I saw a staircase, so I ventured up. The second floor had an entirely separate kitchen and living space and was just as mismatched and dirty as the first floor. *Where in the hell am I? Can I live for three months here on the set of* The Grapes of Wrath? *Is it too late to run?* Then I heard a door open, and a very attractive man entered the kitchen with wet hair, wearing only a towel. Initially what I saw was a young Johnny Depp, and then I quickly realized he was more like a current-day Skeet Ulrich, which, in 1998, actually *was* a version of a young Johnny Depp. His wet torso and this game of Celebrity Look-Alike shook me out of my panic. "Hi! I'm Steve!" this person said.

"Hi. I'm Andrew," I managed to say, though in my head I was chanting, *Please be gay. Please be gay. Please be gay.*

"Sorry I'm running a little late. We are going to see the show tonight, right?"

"I guess so," I said. "I don't really know where we are going though."

"It's just down the road," Steve said. "Let me show you where your bedroom is."

Steve's combination of confidence and blind swagger made me feel certain he was not a gay person but rather just a straight actor who liked to be admired. I felt like we were seconds away from him showing me his dick and saying, "Do you like this? Because you can't have it. But it's nice, right?"

Steve walked me to a small back bedroom with two twin beds. "You'll have to share with Jeff. He seems cool. He's in *Tintypes*." *Everyone needs to stop saying "Tintypes"!* I screamed in my head.

Steve got dressed, and I changed into a slightly different version of what I was already wearing for this "opening night" we were about to attend. We walked to the theater together, down a dirt road and through an empty field. Steve talked the entire time, about where he was from, where he wanted to live in Manhattan, what he was doing for the rest of his summer, and his girlfriend in South Carolina (I was right— straight actor). On top of being handsome, Steve was nice, very nice. I was relieved to have met someone who seemed like he could be a friend.

The inside of the Theater Barn looked more like a theater than a barn, but it still smelled like a barn. There were small glasses of warm white wine on a table in the lobby to celebrate the opening night. Steve and I quickly slammed two each before heading to our seats. As soon as I sat down, a day of travel and anxiety and cheap wine hit me all at once. I was exhausted. I couldn't help but doze off throughout the show. I still couldn't tell you what *Tintypes* is about. I know Theodore Roosevelt showed up at some point and there was a suffragette number. It was a revue, I guess, of songs from early-ish America. I was too tired to really pay attention. But I do remember thinking, *That's going to be me on that stage in two weeks. I will be up there having my own opening night with members of the next cast sitting here, judging me.* I checked my judgment. This cast probably didn't know what *Tintypes* was about, either.

After the show, there was a party, but I was too beat to go. I slipped out of the theater and walked back to the house, through the field and down the dirt road, alone. It was quiet, and a little scary, but pretty. I had never really been in the country like this. The moon was so bright. I remember thinking, *Oh, that's moonlight! It actually does give off a lot of light!* (For those of you thinking, How did he not know this? He's from the prairie, let me clarify: I am from the big city of Omaha, Nebraska, okay? There are tall buildings and hookers and streetlights and everything!)

I got back to the house and realized that it was left open. The doors didn't lock at all. I started to have visions of *In Cold Blood*, but I was too tired to worry about getting murdered that night. I went up to my little shared room and lay down on my bed. A bright overhead light was on above me. *It might be rude to turn that off before my roommate gets home,* I thought. So I fell asleep, fully dressed, with the lights on. My roommate probably thought I *had* been murdered when he finally got home that night.

I woke up the next morning unsure of where I was. I looked around the room and then reality set back in. My roommate was asleep across from me. It was jarring to see a stranger in his underwear so close to my bed. I tiptoed out of my room and into the bathroom, and was startled to hear voices downstairs. I could tell that one was Steve's and the other was a woman's. I went downstairs, and there in the kitchen were Steve, once again in his "Welcome to the House" towel (which made me feel less special), and a young woman with curly brown hair and a megawatt smile. She just looked like sunshine and happiness, and there was something cosmic or past-life about her that I knew I instantly loved. She spotted me. "Are you Andrew? I'm Jenn Gambatese! Your Luisa!" (Luisa and Matt are the star-crossed lovers at the heart of *The Fantasticks*.) She hugged me, and somehow I knew that this summer was going to be okay.

I quickly learned that there is no time for leisure in summer stock. We were at the theater within the hour and reading through the script with the rest of the cast. If you don't know *The Fantasticks*, it is a sweet show written in the sixties by Tom Jones (not that one, though it's fun to imagine . . .) and Harvey Schmidt. It is a simple story about love and loss and learning that, most of the time, what you truly want has been there all along—in this show's case, literally in the characters' own backyard. El Gallo is the narrator and antagonist, Matt and Luisa are the lovers, they each have a father, and there's an old actor character and his assistant and a character called "The Mute" whose primary role is to move scenery around. It's definitely weird, but also incredibly moving, and has gorgeous music in it.

We learned on that first day of rehearsals that instead of fathers, Matt and Luisa would have mothers in this production. (Progressive!) And The Mute would also be played by a woman. (Doubly progressive!) The Mute would be joining us later in the rehearsal process, and everyone else in this cast was a local actor who lived in the area. This was shocking to me at first, but then I learned that a lot of New York City folks have houses in the Berkshires and live there for the summer. The cast was a real grab bag of ages and experience. The mothers both had acting careers in New York, but the old actor and his assistant were truly locals. They were both full-time teachers who just liked acting for fun. So this was part summer stock, part community theater.

The director was a young guy named Brett who took himself very seriously and acted as if we were performing *The Fantasticks* for the first time in American theater history. Even as an inexperienced nineteen-year-old, I immediately had the instinct to roll my eyes at him. But as we read the script for the first time, I was so pleased and excited to find that everyone in the cast was really talented, especially Jenn and Steve. All my anxiety about sharing bedrooms or getting murdered at night because of a home invasion drifted away. I was going to be a serious actor with other serious actors this summer.

The rehearsals for these summer stock productions are sort of a blur. Everyone has to move quickly because you really only have about ten days to put the whole show together before you have an audience. As I said, I had done this particular show two times before, so I already knew the entire thing backward and forward. I would like to say that I was still open to direction, but that would be a lie. I had made my choices and my portrayal of Matt was LOCKED DOWN. This wasn't about "exploring," this was about showing off what I had already discovered. My trick in this show was that I made the bold choice to cry *a lot* at the end. When Matt and Luisa discover they have been in love all along, and what they truly want is to be together, I would launch into a full-out breakdown à la Sally Field in *Steel Magnolias*. It was highly uncalled for, but it made me feel like, well, Sally Field in *Steel Magnolias*, and I loved it.

The big takeaway from rehearsals was that I was working with professionals now. These people came prepared, had ideas, and asked questions that went beyond "Where do I stand?" and "What face do I make?" They were young, but they were ambitious. It made me excited *and* scared. (You're welcome, *Into the Woods* fans.)

Along the way, Steve, Jenn, and I became a tight team. We ate every meal together, we went running together, we stayed up late and drank bad wine together. We grocery shopped together, we did laundry together, we drove around at night and found old cemeteries to walk through together. We were a unit that depended on one another for survival. At least I certainly depended on them. I now know it has to do with the fact that we were spending every waking moment with one another and shared an ambition that clearly stretched beyond the Theater Barn. There was nothing sexual about our attraction, but I fell madly in love with both of them in about three days.

However, I did long for a sexual connection that summer. My maybe-gay liberal arts unicorn, Chris, and I had broken up after classes ended, and I was hopeful that I might be able to find some romance in the Berkshires. I think most actors would agree that there is a game we all play the first day of any rehearsal process. It's called "Who Is Going to Be My

Show Crush?" First, you scan the room looking for someone to flirt with and maybe, one night after a cast party, make out with (at least). Most of the time, you scan the room and find no one. Then, three or four days into rehearsal, everyone starts to look different and suddenly you spot your show crush. He was there all along; it just took time and boredom to find him. Mine came in the shape of our director, Brett. I didn't even particularly care for him, nor did I think he was a great director, but toward the end of our first week, I noticed I was getting some extra attention from him. He liked everything I did in rehearsal and I often caught him staring at me. He was cute in a nerdy way, and I thought, *Why not?!* So I started staring and flirting back. It seemed harmless and added a layer of excitement to my days.

Another fun game actors like to play is "What Can We Complain About Now?" You usually start playing it early in the production process, when everyone is still humbled and grateful for the job and the experience. But slowly, one night after rehearsal and a couple drinks, someone starts complaining about the show, the theater, the director, another cast member. This usually comes from boredom, insecurity, or the desire to find a common enemy. Once the genie is out of the bottle, you can't put him back in. It's a great bonding tool for actors, but if taken too far, it can poison the whole production. With Jenn and Steve, most of the grumbling was about how busted the theater was and what a terrible director Brett was. This put me in an awkward position since I was also flirting with Brett every day. But because I didn't trust his instincts, I also didn't allow him to direct anything I was doing on stage, so I felt like it was fine to gripe about him, too. What this complaining did for me was make me feel (a) closer to Jenn and Steve and (b) like I wanted out of the Theater Barn immediately. I was the only one of the three of us who was staying for the rest of the season, and now I was seriously regretting that choice.

Still, opening night was pretty magical, as I recall. I was on stage with people I loved, and what's more, I was in love with their talent. As Jenn and Steve and I performed the final moments of that show together, I felt that we were doing good work, and that I was sharing this space, this stage, with people who were making me a better actor. When I cried at the end of the show that first night, it wasn't my usual up-staging sobs. I just looked at Jenn, happy for her friendship and amazed by her abilities and cried appropriate, authentic tears of joy.

This rush of emotion was met with a near immediate crash when I realized that we only had two weeks together before Jenn and Steve would leave and I would be left alone with a new cast to start rehearsals for *Forever Plaid*. I tried to put this thought out of my head, and by that I mean, I drowned my sadness in Franzia white wine at the cast party at Joan's house later that night. I stayed close to Jenn and Steve, trying to soak in every moment with them.

At one point, while I was tipping a box of wine into my Solo cup, Brett approached me. He, too, had been enjoying the Franzia and was now bold enough to tell me how much he liked me. He talked about how talented and funny and handsome I was. Before I knew it, I was agreeing to meet him in his bedroom after the party. But there was a catch. He was staying in Joan's house, and he didn't want her to know that we were "spending time together." I suggested my house. He said that was a bad idea since there were so many people there. I couldn't argue with that. "What should we do?" I asked. (This is where, dear reader, you will see just how little self-esteem Andy Rannells had at this point and also what a ridiculous romantic he was.) Brett suggested that I go home with Jenn and Steve and wait until they were asleep. Then, I would sneak out of our house, walk through the fields to Joan's house, and go to Brett's bedroom window at the back, where I would stand on Joan's central air-conditioning unit and hoist myself through said window and into his bedroom. I thought about this plan. The lying, the plotting, the potential danger/humiliation. Then I said, "Okay!" It sounded tricky but fun. I would be like Romeo climbing through Juliet's window!

I went with Jenn and Steve back to the house, where we drank and talked and drank more. Once back in our house, I didn't want to leave. I wanted to stay with them. But I had made a plan, and my Midwestern politeness, not to mention my penis, was not going to let me forget it. After some fake yawning, I said my good-nights and made my way to my bedroom. I snuck out the back door and walked quietly down the road, through the fields to Joan's house. The moonlight was once again bright enough to light my way. I got to the house and, as planned, Brett had his window open. Getting through the window was a little harder than I had expected, but I did it. Brett acted as if this was something we did all the time. He seemed almost bored with my arrival. "Where have you been?" he asked tersely.

"I had to wait for Jenn and Steve to go to sleep."

"I thought you weren't coming. I almost went to bed."

I was suddenly feeling punished. This wasn't even my idea. I didn't even really care about being here. But I stayed. We had sex. It was fun, I guess. Good, I guess. And totally silent. He told me I couldn't make any noise for fear that Joan would hear. It added a level of excitement, I guess. (I'm sure "Silent Sex" is something that has been fetishized and discussed on an episode of *Real Sex* on HBO at some point.) He came, I didn't, and without the power of speech, I couldn't correctly charade, "Hey, what about me?" Before I knew it, Brett was asleep and I was lying in his bed, in the dark, wondering why I was there. I knew why he'd invited me, but why did I go? I drifted asleep and awoke to Brett fully dressed and packing his suitcase.

"Good morning," he said. "That was fun."

I gestured silently to the bedroom door. "Is Joan here?"

"She went to the grocery store. This is probably a good time to sneak out. I have to leave soon anyway."

Being asked to leave, or rather "sneak out," is not the most pleasant way to be greeted in the morning. But being a polite guy with limited experience (or just a dummy), I started to dress quickly.

"Are you coming back anytime soon?" I asked, foolishly.

"I have jobs lined up for the rest of the summer, but I will try. Truly. I'd like to do this again, Andrew."

I smiled like an idiot. Then Brett's face got serious. "Andrew, I think I told you this, but I have a boyfriend, so can you not mention this to Jenn or Steve?"

No, no Brett, you certainly didn't mention the boyfriend. Also, I will definitely be telling Jenn and Steve. But what I said was "Of course." We hugged good-bye and then I quickly left the house.

I walked back through the fields in my opening night outfit wondering why I had done that to myself. Was it fun? Did I like it? Did I like him? Yes? No? A little, I guess. I approached the house. It looked prettier in the early morning light than it did normally. I looked around at the fields and the trees and thought, *Where in the hell am I? I am doing theater in the middle of a goddamn farm with a bunch of strangers and I just had sex with one of them. I am stuck here for the whole rest of the summer. I want out! I want to go back to New York right now! How can I get out of this?*

I sat down on the porch and tried to calm myself. I was still doing a show I loved with people I loved, and I was getting better as an actor from working out here. Also, I reminded myself, I had been hired as an actor in New York City out of hundreds of other actors who had auditioned. *I was picked.* And if I was picked this time, there would definitely be a next time. My acting career had begun. It might have begun in a barn performing for grouchy-looking farmers, but it had begun. And sometimes just getting started is enough. In that sense, I guess my acting teacher was right; summer stock was indeed some of the best training for a young actor.

Young Artists Seeking . . . Art

I DISCOVERED TWO IMPORTANT THINGS DURING MY summer on a musical theater farm in upstate New York: (1) The difference between The City and The Country was as extreme as visiting a different planet. (2) I am most definitely a City person. I had just about clicked into the rhythm of the city when I had been uprooted by my Theater Barn detour, and I was beyond excited to be back to the business of turning myself into Eustace Tilley.

My dreams of living in New York went beyond Broadway and the appeal of wearing all-black clothing; I wanted the whole lifestyle that came with being a New Yorker. I wanted to walk into a deli with my MoMA tote bag, complain about subway service intelligently, and order myself a "regular coffee" and understand exactly what I was getting. (That's with milk, two sugars.) But perhaps most of all, I wanted to be a cultured person in the way I perceived New Yorkers to be. I wanted to go to art galleries and performance installations and plays that were staged in abandoned storefronts. My partner in this exploration was always Zuzanna. We were young artists. We were living in New York City now. There were experiences to be had. There was art to be seen. And we were going to find it all. After years of being limited to community theater productions and big-screen blockbusters in the Midwest, we were hungry for darker fare. We wanted to be *challenged*. In short, we wanted to see some weird shit.

Even though we were new to the city, we somehow knew that the key to finding what we were looking for lay in the *Village Voice*. Every week it was dense with the kind of counterculture events that we wanted to be a part of. TKTS, the half-price ticket booth, was great for Broadway shows and even off-Broadway shows, and I visited often. ("One ticket for *The Life*, please!") But Zuzanna and I wanted some theater off the beaten path, far from Broadway and its mainstream shine. Our first outing took us to Theater for the New City, deep in the East Village, on First Avenue and 10th Street. I'll be honest, as I recall we based this choice on two factors: Tickets were not only available, but also only $10, and the title of the show was *Sex Industry*. It was advertised as a gritty portrayal of female sex workers in America. It sounded potentially moving and maybe political. Seemed like a good bet. Plus, we liked hanging out in the East Village. There was a drag bar we'd discovered on St. Marks and Avenue A called Stingy Lulu's. Not only did they not card, but it was fun and colorful, and all the waitresses were drag queens who did numbers in between delivering cocktails. There was certainly nothing like it in Omaha. The plan was to see the show and then have drinks at Stingy Lulu's. Even if the show was bad, we could turn the night around with our drag friends.

The theater itself didn't look like any theater I had ever been to. The lobby looked more like a Bohemian rummage sale. There was broken furniture and pieces of past sets strewn about, and almost everything was covered with some kind of sheer fabric or sheet. It smelled like incense, and I'm fairly certain I saw a cat or two running about. The doors to the house weren't open yet, and everyone was just milling about in the lobby. They had a card table set up with free wine. (Free wine was becoming a warning of sorts. If you walk into a theater and there is free wine, consider it a preemptive apology, or at least a distraction. And always drink it.) We helped ourselves and took in the crowd. It was a lively group of various ages. Everyone had a real East Village vibe, which at the time was chic in a slightly un-ironed and potentially smelly way. (My most distinct sense memory is a lot of patchouli and a residual weed-smoking stench.)

The theater had open seating, or "festival seating" as it is sometimes optimistically called, so once the doors to the theater were opened, you just had to sort of shove your way in and fight for seats. We beelined it up to the back row. We felt it would be safer in case the show was a total disaster and we wanted to leave, or if there was some kind of unexpected audience participation. (I have always hated interactive theater. I don't mean immersive theater; I loved *Natasha, Pierre and The Great Comet of 1812*. I mean interactive theater, like when you have to participate and actors touch you and want you to speak to them. I'm sorry, but if I wanted to be in the show, I would have auditioned for it.)

To the best of my recollection, *Sex Industry* was a series of vignettes about women who worked as strippers or prostitutes in New York City. The dialogue wasn't written as traditional dialogue but rather as a bizarre style of poetry. There was a lot of repeating of words and phrases and rhythmic talking. It wasn't like Beat poetry, which might have been cool, this

seemed more like . . . an accident or a struggle to remember
one's lines. Zuzanna and I tried to follow the story until we
realized that there wasn't one. I think we both tapped out
when one of the actresses delivered an impassioned monologue about that fact that she often had to defecate after sex.
That was pretty much the point when we decided our outing
was a bit of a misfire. But *Sex Industry* would not deter us!
We would try again!

Zuzanna was taking a Theater History class at Barnard,
and she would receive extra credit for seeing certain performances that weren't affiliated with her school. Because
Zuzanna loved extra credit, and I loved hanging out with
Zuzanna, I told her I would join her for one of these performances. The next one coming up was an avant-garde, modern Chinese opera. Check, check, and check in my book!
That sounded like a perfect, and maybe oddly cool, way to
spend the afternoon. The title, which was in Chinese obviously, translated to *The Woman with the Glass Vagina*. Once
again I was reminded that I was NOT in Omaha. The show,
a matinee, was at the Asia Society. The audience was mostly
made up of affluent-looking Chinese folks with a handful of
students like us sprinkled in. As we were entering the theater,
an usher asked us, "Do you speak Chinese?"

"Sadly, no, we do not," I said.

"That's okay, you can use these headsets. We have a translator today."

Just our luck! I had only ever seen two operas in my life
at that point, so I was prepared for the traditional supertitles
above the stage used to translate the lyrics. But headsets? This
was way more fun! We settled into our seats and the opera

began. The translator, who I had thought would be a fun addition to the experience, turned out to be very distracting. It was a woman with a monotone voice, reading what seemed like a very literal translation of what was being sung. So while listening to the performers on stage sing, there was a woman in our ears in a low voice, like a female Ben Stein, saying things like:

Can't you see my vagina is made of glass? Look. It's glass. It is a glass vagina.

I'm sure it sounded more poetic in Chinese.

The climax of the show came a painstaking two hours later when the lead character—the one with the aforementioned glass vagina—had sex for the first time and, you guessed it, her glass vagina shattered into a million pieces. Honestly, the effect was really amazing. The actress was sitting on top of something that looked like a really, really long playground slide, her legs straddling either side. Then, when her poor vagina broke, countless, I mean, *countless*, marbles were poured down the slide between her legs. It went on for quite some time, all while the chorus was singing around her and the translator kept droning in our ears:

Her vagina is broken. She has broken her glass vagina.

All in all, not a total theatrical slam-dunk for Zuzanna and me. But some parts were cool and it got me out of my dorm room and it got Zuzanna some extra credit.

After that, we decided that maybe the cinema was a safer bet. We branched out of the live theater scene and looked for some fun, indie, art house films that could be inspiring. I decided to spearhead this new effort and once again took to the *Village Voice* for guidance. There were so many movies I had never heard of, so many movie houses I had never been to. I was getting excited about this next adventure. The options seemed limitless. For example, a Truffaut retrospective? At the time I didn't know who that was, but it sounded French and arty. How about *Following* from up-and-coming director Christopher Nolan? I think it's in black-and-white! That's fun! No, I decided to let my penis be the guide and chose a film purely based on its poster. It was called *Latin Boys Go to Hell*. (Google it. Gays and girls, you're welcome.) I didn't read a synopsis, I just figured that if the guy on the poster was in the movie, that was good enough for me! It was playing at the Quad, a small theater on 13th Street that Zuzanna and I had never been to. The theater was packed with older West Village gay men and us. Today, the internet describes the film's plot as such: "Young Brooklyn Latinos learn about the intricacies of relationships and their own developing sexuality."

What I remember about it was there was a lot of nudity, a lot of overacting, and then the hot guy from the poster gets his penis cut off. (What was it with us finding all these stories about damage to the genitals?) The movie ended and I knew I had led us astray. Luckily Zuzanna found that castrated poster guy attractive, too, so ultimately, all was not lost.

Our search was never ending. There was never a shortage of things to see, experiences to seek out. And yet we usually managed to just miss the thing that everyone else was raving about. We never discovered the next *Rent* or *Little Shop of Horrors*. There was no *Hamilton* that we stumbled on while trying to experience unexpected art in the city. But we had successes. I remember seeing the Todd Solondz film *Hap-*

piness with Zuzanna and being part of a small handful of people left in the theater when it was over, after several scenes made people walk out in droves. (We loved it.) We saw Uta Hagen in *Collected Stories* at the Lucille Lortel Theatre. She was as incredible as we had hoped she'd be. And we saw the revival of *Cabaret* with Alan Cumming, Natasha Richardson, and John Benjamin Hickey. (I know it's a Broadway show, but the theater was super-run-down and *east* of Broadway so it felt more downtown.) It's still one of my favorite theatrical experiences ever. We were happy to take them all as they came.

There was always a lot of amazing art to discover in New York. And lucky for us, there was also always a lot of weird shit. The best part was we were always surrounded by other New Yorkers. And slowly but surely, we were becoming New Yorkers ourselves.

We also learned that I am too tall to comfortably carry a tote bag and I don't like sugar in my coffee. We were finding our way.

Josephine

I GUESS IT WOULD HAVE BEEN AROUND THE EIGHTH grade when I started hearing the first grumblings about my grandma Josephine "forgetting things." I can only accurately date events from my Nebraska years by thinking back to which community theater production I was in at the time. I believe this would have been just after my groundbreaking performance—at least in my mind—in an original play at Creighton University called *Doin' Chickens*. I played a young boy in the Appalachian Mountains who dreamed of getting off the farm, only to have his family terrorized by local thugs. It was very long, very bloody, and very violent, and to this day my mother is still traumatized when we discuss it. Why my parents let me be in it in the first place is a mystery. I think they just liked that I wasn't watching *Dirty Dancing* on a loop anymore. Either way, the show was my personal *Sophie's Choice*. I acted so hard, my face hurt. The *Omaha World Herald* called my Appalachian accent "convincing." (I just watched *Coal Miner's Daughter* on repeat until I sounded like Sissy Spacek.) Usually Josephine would attend every show I was in, but I didn't tell her about *Doin' Chickens*. With all the blood and rape, it didn't seem very "grandma friendly." She probably wouldn't have noticed all the violence since she usually fell asleep the second the lights went out. But it always meant a lot that she came to support me.

It was around this time when the frowning faces and whispering behind Josephine's back began. She seemed fine to me. I guess I just assumed that it was totally normal for older people to start forgetting where certain pieces of china were kept or which grandkid belonged to which child. I mean, the woman had a lot of grandkids. I would forget a couple, too. I was also in denial. I didn't want anything to be wrong with her. She was my only grandparent left. The panic about Josephine, in my opinion, seemed premature. But apparently some doctor started using the "A" word and everyone lost their shit.

Alzheimer's.

A word that immediately strikes panic into the heart and mind of everyone. And thanks to that Julianne Moore movie a few years ago, we now know we can get it while we are still youngish and pretty.

Given Josephine's diagnosis, I thought that she should move in with us. After all, my mother talked often, and fondly, about what a gift it had been to grow up with her own grandmother living in her house. But I was only fourteen at the time, and I didn't realize how much work that would have been, not to mention how much stress it would have put on my parents' marriage. So a nurse was hired to take care of Josephine in her home during the week. My mom and her siblings would take turns staying with her on the weekends.

I started to see Josephine fading a bit, but only in glimpses. For the most part, she was still the strong, funny woman I had always known. The woman who would stay up nearly all night in the days close to Easter to make Lamb Cakes for family and friends. To clarify, Lamb Cakes are not cakes made of *actual* lamb; they are cakes made in the *shape* of a lamb. The cake itself is a dense white or prune cake that you bake in a cast-iron mold shaped like a lamb lying daintily on its side. Then you frost the hell out of it and cover it in flaked coconut to make it look like wool. If I am being honest, I never really cared for Lamb Cakes, but Josephine worked so hard on them that we were always forced to choke a piece down. Sometimes two if you were sitting next to her.

Josephine also taught me how to gossip in church and other public places. She really mastered the "talking shit through your teeth" thing. She would smile and smile, all while telling you about someone's daughter who got knocked up or how fat someone had gotten. She could have been a ventriloquist. She was that good.

She also taught me how to throw shade. For example, if it was a little chilly outside and she saw a mother with a baby who, in her opinion, was not wearing proper outdoor clothing, she would stop and smile at the baby and then in a sweet old lady voice say, "Well, aren't you precious? It's too bad your mother didn't pack a coat and hat for you today. You are going to get sick, poor thing."

Josephine was a shady lady but classy—always well-dressed, hair and makeup done. Occasionally she would bust out a bright wig she had purchased in the seventies, which was a little jarring, but I always appreciated the effort. It was like she was playing herself in a stage production of her life.

She was also incredibly loving and supportive. I remember playing in her house with my sister Julie and my cousin Tom when I was six. Our game involved pretending Josephine's La-Z-Boy recliner was a rocket of some sort. We were throwing up the footrest while simultaneously slamming back the chair into full recline mode and making rocket noises and screaming. My memory is slightly hazy about who was actually in the chair at the time (that's not true; it was totally Julie), but on one such rocket trip, the chair spun and knocked a lamp to the ground. It didn't break, but we ripped the hell out of the shade. Hearing the racket, adults, including my grandmother, rushed into the room. I somehow was blamed. (I love Julie, but she was never afraid to throw you under the bus. She could be very sweet, but she could also turn on you in a second. At this age she strongly resembled Tina Yothers from *Family Ties* but acted more like Donna Mills on *Knots Landing*.)

I ran crying into my grandmother's bedroom to hide out for a bit. My mom was never a yeller, but she followed me into the room and simply told me in a very "Faye Dunaway as Joan Crawford" tone that she was "very disappointed" in me. I sat there crying in Josephine's bedroom, feeling like I was the worst person in the world. After a couple minutes, Josephine came in and sat next to me on the bed. "Andy," she said, "I don't care about that lamp. It was an accident, I know that. It's okay. I love you." And then she hugged me until I stopped crying.

So looking at her now, in the same house where she had always lived, hosting Christmas Eve dinners and Easter egg hunts, all I saw was the same lady I had always loved. Sure, she was a little slower, but she still got there. If anything she just seemed a little, I don't know, lonely, I guess. Maybe a little sadder than I had seen her. Years went by like this. Mostly good moments, some not so good, but in my mind she was doing okay. I was, at this point, a senior in high school and very busy with the typical teenage nonsense, but something within me knew that it was important to keep up my own relationship with my grandma. I started visiting her after school, bringing her flowers or little gifts. She seemed happy to see me.

It was on one such visit that my grandma called me "Frank." I just let it go; she could call me whatever she wanted. But it kept happening—she would mostly address me as "Frank." I finally asked my mom if there was a Frank in our family. She thought about it for a while and then she said, "Frank was the man your grandma was dating before she married your grandfather." So Josephine thought I was her old boyfriend. It was a little creepy, but it made sense. Here I was, visiting her often and bringing her gifts and flowers; she assumed that I was wooing her in some way. I didn't mind. At least she was always happy to see me. Frank must have been a good guy, because she liked Frank, I mean, me. We had good visits—that was the important thing.

And then one afternoon, I visited and Josephine was not in her La-Z-Boy by the window. I asked her nurse where she was. "Oh, your grandma is not having a good day," she said. "She's in her bedroom, but I wouldn't go in there." I didn't listen. I walked into her bedroom and it was dark, with the curtains drawn. Josephine was sitting on the edge of her bed, sort of hunched over. "Go away," she said.

"Grandma," I said, "it's me." She looked up at me and started to cry.

"Oh Andy. Something is very wrong."

I was startled. She hadn't said my name in months and I hadn't seen her cry in many years. I sat down on the bed next to her. "What's wrong, Grandma?"

"There's a woman out there and I don't know who she is. I know she is supposed to be here, but I don't know why. Why is she in my house? I know there is something wrong with me, but I don't know what it is. What's wrong with me? Why can't I remember what's wrong?"

She continued to cry, softly at first, and then harder and harder. I didn't know what to do. I had heard my mother talk about the fact that some days, Josephine would have moments of total clarity, that she would remember where she was and who everyone was around her. This was almost one of those moments, but not quite. It seemed to me the most terrifying state of all: sure of yourself, your body, your home, but not quite as sure of how you got there. Like when you go on vacation and you wake up in the middle of the night in a dark hotel room, and maybe for a split second you don't know where you are. You know you are *you*, and yet your surroundings are completely foreign and a little scary. But that moment only lasts a couple of seconds. You piece together the geography of the room, you see your suitcase, you see the alarm clock, and it starts to come back in a flash: You are on vacation, this is your hotel room. You feel sane again, you feel safe, you can fall back to sleep. Josephine couldn't piece anything together. She was trying and trying to make sense of the math of the house, but she couldn't quite solve it. It was so close, it was all right there, but it just wouldn't add up.

What could I do? Do I tell her she's sick? Do I tell her

that the woman in the living room is a nurse, and has been staying with her for years? Do I tell her I'm sorry? That I love her? That it will all be okay? It wasn't okay, she wasn't okay, and she wouldn't be okay. It came crashing down on me all at once that she was ill, seriously ill, and I couldn't do anything to change that. Now it was my turn to try and comfort her. I put my arm around her and I held her. She cried. And then I cried. We sat on that bed and just held each other for a long time. Then like a fog lifting, she sat up straight and looked at me with a soft but vague expression. "Hello," she said. She was gone again. Her one moment of clarity that day, that week, that month, was gone and it had been spent in terror, in sadness. I felt awful and yet relieved that she was calm again at least. I hated myself for not knowing what to do in that moment. I never told anyone about that visit. I didn't want to admit that it had happened.

Shortly after that, she moved into a nursing home. She was getting worse, angry, too hard to control. So she would live in a home with strangers, sleeping next to strangers, eating next to strangers. Did she know? Did she care? I cared very much. I would think of her in that home, and I would imagine her having one of those moments that she'd had with me, a moment of realizing that she was still herself. It killed me to think of her waking up at night in a strange room, with a stranger sleeping just a few feet away. She would be terrified. Sometimes, to selfishly comfort myself, I would imagine that perhaps her moment of clarity and her roommate's moment of clarity would coincide. That these two women who used to be fully functioning adults in the world would look at each other and just say, "Where the fuck are we? What the fuck is going on here?" Maybe they would laugh, probably they would cry, but at least they wouldn't be totally alone. I suspect that's not the way it works.

I couldn't say for sure, though, because I never visited my grandma at the nursing home. I had just moved to New York and was wrapped up in getting settled and creating a space for myself there. While I barely made it home that first year, I'm disappointed in myself for not making more of an effort to see her when I did. Phone calls weren't possible; she would never have known who I was on the phone. I missed her and thought of her often, but I wondered if she ever thought of me. Maybe, but probably not. I didn't blame her.

While I was slinging back G&Ts at Rose's Turn, suffering my way through summer stock, and seeing a lot of questionable theater with Zuzanna, I had let a lot of relationships with my family slip. It wasn't intentional. Or maybe it was. I was homesick, a feeling that I had privately vowed to never experience. I knew that I belonged in New York, that Omaha wasn't the right place for me anymore, so how could I possibly miss so much about it? I missed my family, I missed our home, I missed dinners and holidays and trips to the mall. But it hurt to think about those things. It was easier to forget. So I decided to not acknowledge those feelings; I just pushed them aside like I did with so many other thoughts that came into my head those first years away from home. It hurt to hang up the phone, so I called less. It hurt to leave after a visit, so I visited less. My relationships were suffering, and as my grandma got sicker and sicker, that reality hit me. I had played this all wrong. It was the wrong strategy for homesickness. I couldn't let myself do that anymore.

Almost a year after Josephine moved into the home, she

died. She died in a bedroom that was not her own, surrounded by strangers. I can only hope that in the moments before she went, she was in a haze of some sort of contentment and not confusion. I hope it was soft. I hope it was calm. I hope there was no panic.

I came home from college for the funeral. It was a terribly somber event. My mother and her siblings had started fighting quite a bit after my grandmother got sick. There were disagreements about how she should be cared for and unresolved tensions about their pasts. These created a divide that would take years to heal. I tried to remember what that all looked like, hoping that my siblings and I would not make the same mistakes when it came time to care for our parents. I sat next to my sister Natalie at the church, both of us unsure what to say about anything.

I thought about Josephine, lying in that coffin, surrounded by loved ones weeping for her. I thought about her final years and how unfair it all was that it ended so badly. Then I thought about all the times I had sat next to Josephine at various funerals and weddings and baptisms. All the receptions and luncheons we had gone to together. The holidays and birthdays and Sunday dinners. The Lamb Cakes and the Polish sausage made. The stories told. Josephine could teach you to curse in Polish and also tell you everything about the lives of the saints of the Catholic Church. She was a woman who raised five children in a two-bedroom house. She was strong and resourceful and creative. She had fourteen grandchildren and she made them all feel special and loved, each in a unique way. Her life was more than the last few years. It was mostly joyous and filled with love.

I looked around the room at all the relatives divided by

this disease and by fear and sadness. What would Josephine do if she were here with us? She could fix this, she could lift this cloud. I leaned over to Natalie and through a smile I said, "Aunt Kathy looks like a hooker in that dress."

Natalie looked at me a little stunned but then instantly knew. "And did you see Christine? She's fat as a house now."

So that's what we did. We sat through that whole funeral making fun of our relatives. I think Josephine would have wanted it that way.

Broadway Adjacent

WHEN I GOT BACK FROM THE THEATER BARN, I knew I was capable of booking professional work—albeit work that was contingent upon my willingness to also clean the urinals in the men's room—and yet here I was starting another semester at a school I wasn't happy with and spending time, energy, and my limited funds on a degree that I wasn't sure was necessary for my future. Most of the people I had just worked with in summer stock had college degrees and were making the same $150 a week I was. Did I need a degree to be an actor? Was it something that I had to have to work? Was I really learning anything useful?

Making things worse, my teen modeling savings were nearly gone. My tuition was paid for, but I still had to pay for room and board and general living expenses, and New York had proven to be way more expensive than I had planned. (He said to the surprise of no one.) I started classes again and went through the motions of being a student. I was waking up with financial panic attacks almost daily, and I was skipping most of my classes to make time for work, which, looking back, seems insane since I was skipping the thing that I was trying to pay for.

I had two part-time jobs. The first was at Equinox gym,

as a front desk clerk. I took this job mainly so I could get the free membership that came with it. It was easy work; I just had to check people in as they entered. It was pretty uneventful, except for the occasional entitled Upper East Sider who would burst into the gym with no membership card and no ID, and insist that I should remember his or her face and name. In those instances I would usually fold and just let the person in, but depending on my mood, I would sometimes punish those rich people by making them spell their names *very* slowly for me while I searched for their membership folder. I have to say that a real highlight of that job was that every once in a while Isabella Rossellini would come in. She never had her ID, but she was always incredibly polite and would voluntarily spell her first and last name so I could check her in. And she always apologized for not bringing her ID card. I will always love her for that.

My second job was more soul-crushing. I was a greeter at the Warner Bros. store. "Why was that so bad?" you ask. I'll tell you. The Warner Bros. store was eight floors of merchandise packed into a sterile high-rise on the corner of 57th and Fifth Avenue. T-shirts, hats, flatware, glasses, jewelry, DVDs—anything any Warner Bros. fan could dream of— even Tweety Bird mud flaps. (That is not a joke. We sold those.) All I had to do was stand in front of the entrance and welcome people into the store by saying, "Welcome to the Warner Bros. store! Eight floors of fun!" Sometimes I would say, "Eight floors of stuff!" just to prove to myself that no one was paying attention to me. At least Isabella Rossellini remembered my name.

Then one day, like a magical rope that dropped into my

self-indulgent pit of despair, I saw a notice for an audition in *Backstage* that I was certain would fix all my problems. It contained two phrases that filled me with incredible hope: "*Grease—The Musical*" and "Dinner Theater." This was perfect! I had just played Doody in summer stock to great acclaim—one Berkshire newspaper had called me "tall and blonde"—and most of my acting experience was in dinner theater. (Please recall my run in *On Golden Pond* at thirteen years old.) I didn't even know New York had dinner theaters; they seemed like such a Midwestern thing. This one was called the Westchester Broadway Theatre. The name was a little paradoxical. How could it be both Broadway *and* dinner theater? I told myself I'd worry about that later.

The day of the audition I called in sick to both of my jobs and spent all day waiting in line to grab what was mine. As desperate as I was, I also felt extremely confident. I finally got in the room and sang my song and read my scenes, and was asked to stay and dance. Normally this would have made me nervous because I was never a great dancer, no matter how hard I tried. But in this case I already knew the hand jive from being in *Grease* in the Berkshires, so I was feeling real good. I left that day certain of my fate at the Westchester Broadway Theatre. Soon I would be back singing and dancing in front of crowds slurping down Grasshoppers and Beef Stroganoff, just like they did in Omaha.

Sure enough, two days later I got the call that I had booked the role of Doody. I would receive $400 a week for fourteen weeks of employment, and the best news was that at the end of the contract, I would receive my Actors' Equity card. This meant better jobs, insurance, a pension, and unlimited use of the bathrooms in the Times Square offices. It was way better than I could have imagined!

But now I was faced with a difficult choice: I couldn't do this show and stay in school full-time, nor could I keep my work schedule up, particularly while in rehearsals. What was I going to do? Play it safe or follow my heart back to the dinner theater buffet line? I consulted with no one, I made no list of pros and cons, I didn't even flip a coin. I just impulsively decided to blow up my life and take the show. I dropped out of Marymount, quit both my jobs, and moved out of my dorm and into a small apartment near Columbia University with Zuzanna. I threw caution and all rational judgment to the wind! Moving in with Zuzanna was the start of a whole new adventure. I was a real, struggling actor now. No safety net. The benefit of having my parents *not* help me pay for college was that this was solely my decision to make. I didn't feel like I owed them an explanation or an apology for dropping out. This new adventure would be funded and designed by me.

Rehearsals quickly started and I was in heaven. The cast featured many young people, but I was one of the youngest. There were people who had worked all over the country in national tours, and they seemed so much cooler and wiser. I tried to soak it all in, including the stories of auditions and jobs nearly booked. One of the girls in the show had met Bernadette Peters, for Christ's sake.

And then there was my Danny Zuko. His name was Todd. He was six-foot-four and looked like Lorenzo Lamas and Adrian Zmed had had a sexy man baby. He had just come from the national tour of *Grease*, where he had also played Danny Zuko. He wore tight rehearsal shorts and had long fifties-style black hair. I immediately fell in love with him, but my heart was instantly broken when he told us at lunch one day that he was recently divorced . . . FROM A WOMAN. I was devastated, but I still loved him from afar. I always managed to get myself staged right next to him in scenes and dance numbers, and I successfully worked in a bit of choreography where Danny put Doody in a headlock for no reason. I could feel his washboard abs through his T-shirt. I could have stayed in that headlock forever.

Unrequited romances aside, I was living my best life thanks to the guidance of Oprah and her friend Gary Zukav. I didn't miss Marymount at all, and I was so happy to be getting paid to do what I had always dreamed of doing. There was one big catch, however. As an actor, my math skills were not exactly what they could have been, and $400 a week after taxes in New York City didn't exactly stretch as far as I would have liked. I was often faced with difficult decisions: Lunch or two more vodka sodas after the show? Pay my rent on time or go grocery shopping? Go to the doctor or just take some echinacea and pray? I was often late with my bills and I was always stressed about money, but I was very thin. That had to count for something.

Once the show was up and running, I settled into a comfortable schedule. I'd take a van to Westchester every day, do the show at night, and take that same van back into the city, where I'd party with my cast, sleep off a hangover, and start all over again. I felt like I was part of something, a community of people who had the same goals and dreams that I did. There is an energy, an urgency, to being around people like that. I was motivated to do more and want more. And they were fun. We would go to dive bars in Hell's Kitchen and dance and laugh and gossip about people. We used to play a game at the end of the night where, before last call, we would shout out how much money we had in our checking accounts and whoever had the least would get a free drink. It was usually me, but I remember being genuinely happy anyway.

And then, just as my first taste of contentment settled in, I was reminded of just how far Westchester was from Broadway. My friend Jenn from the Theater Barn booked a Broadway show. She was the first of my friends to do it, and while I was happy for her, I was also suddenly embarrassed. The job I had been so proud of now seemed not good enough. She was going to join the chorus of *Footloose*. The show had gotten terrible reviews, but who cared? She was going to be on Broadway.

It all seemed to move so quickly, and before I knew it, she was out of rehearsals and on stage. I had one night off a week from *Grease* when I could see her perform. Tickets were expensive, but Jenn was able to get me a cheap seat in the front row. It was not a great way to take in the emotionally layered story of *Footloose*, but it was the perfect way to see my dream up close. I really couldn't tell you much about that show; I was too busy tracking Jenn through her every move. I felt a strange combination of pride and jealousy, a mixture of emotions that I would become accustomed to over the next several years. I started looking at other men my age in the chorus. They were all so talented. Could that ever be me? Was I Broadway good or just Westchester Broadway good? By the end of the show I was thrilled for Jenn and depressed for me.

I waited for her at the stage door afterward, and she eventually exited with some of her new Broadway cast friends. There were hugs and handshakes, and then we all went to a diner to grab something to eat. I could only afford to order a Coke, but I sat with them and listened as they talked about the backstage drama at *Footloose*. It was terribly exciting. As I walked Jenn home, she told me she had something important to ask me. *Was there an opening in* Footloose *for me?* I wondered. *Would she be able to lift me out of the Westchester Broadway Theatre?* "You made quite an impression at the show tonight," she said. "Two different guys asked me who you were and if you were single." I was not expecting this development, but suddenly it seemed like a great distraction from my professional angst.

"Which guys?" I asked.

"Willard and Lyle."

Willard was the comic relief character played by Chris Penn in the movie, and Lyle was a chorus member who made a very memorable entrance at one point in the first act in a wrestling singlet. I was torn. Do I go for the featured actor or the guy with the impressive package?

"Which one is nicer?" I asked.

"Well, they both are nice, but Willard had crabs last week. I think you should go for Lyle."

Decision made! I would go on a date with Lyle, whose real name was Jim. I couldn't remember what his face looked like, only the singlet, but how bad could it be? Jenn hatched a plan for me to meet him after our shows one night.

We met up at a dive bar in Hell's Kitchen where the casts of many Broadway shows would hang out. I brought a couple friends from *Grease* as backup in case something went awry.

We were immediately overwhelmed by the number of Broadway chorus kids living it up at this bar. It was a whole new level of post-show partying. Jim/Lyle and I hit it off, and by that I mean we almost immediately started making out. (Dear reader, please keep track of these bar make-outs. This became a real trend for me.) Surrounded by Broadway show folk, kissing a featured chorus member, my head twirled into a new level of consciousness. *Maybe I could get closer to my dream by simply hanging out with other people who were doing what I wanted to be doing. I could just fake it until I actually make it.*

After that first night, Jim/Lyle and I had a whirlwind romance that would carry me through the rest of my run of *Grease.* I was hanging out with his cast all the time, meeting other Broadway actors, going to parties and events, all while singing my heart out as Doody every night at the dinner theater. My part in this professional world was so tiny I was practically invisible, but I also felt like I was finally in the right line. It might be long and winding, and I couldn't really see the end of it, but I knew I was in it.

My second-to-last week of *Grease* I received my Equity card and my weekly salary went from $400 a week to $405, the Equity minimum for that contract. I was going out with a bang! Just when I didn't think things could get better, *Rent* called, this time with an audition for Mark. That was a MUCH better part for me than Angel. I felt like everything was falling into place. All my journaling about my future and my daily affirmations were paying off.

As the last week of my *Grease* contract approached, I went back in for *Rent.* I wore my Calvin Klein carpenter jeans again, this time with a tight Henley and Converse sneakers. I sang BOTH of the given songs this time, and as I left I felt certain that this was going to be my Broadway break. That night after my show, I met up with Jim/Lyle, who looked a little tense.

"I've been meaning to tell you that I'm leaving *Footloose*, Andrew."

This came as a shock. Who would ever want to leave *Footloose*?

"I'm doing a European tour of *West Side Story*. I'm playing Riff!"

I tried to rally some supportive enthusiasm. "Congratulations, Lyle! I mean, Jim! That's so exciting. How long will you be gone?"

Jim/Lyle made an exaggerated sad face. "A year."

My heart sank a bit. I really liked Jim/Lyle. "Oh, okay."

"And there's something else, too . . . I really like you, Andrew. Spending this time with you has made me realize how much I miss my ex-boyfriend. He's going to be playing Baby John on the same tour, so I feel like the universe is telling me to give it another shot with him."

I felt my face get hot. It wasn't that I was about to burst into tears; it was more like I was going to vomit with rage and embarrassment. Jim/Lyle sensed my mood shift.

"I'm really sorry. I think you are really great."

"Thank you. I'm happy for you, Jim," I lied. "When do you leave?"

"Next week."

He really waited until the last minute to spring this on me. I tried to comfort myself by imagining that I would be in *Rent* rehearsals by then anyway. I didn't have time for a Jim or a Lyle; I was going to be learning how to be Mark. Jim took my hand. "Do you still want to have sex tonight, though?"

I was outraged, then aroused, then sad, then lonely, then aroused again, and finally resolved. "Sure," I said. So we did, and that would be the last time I saw Jim/Lyle for a long time.

The final weekend of *Grease* performances began, and while I was sad about Jim/Lyle, I brushed it off and tried to focus on having fun with my cast while awaiting a life-changing call from *Rent*. *Grease* closed on a Sunday night and we all got drunk as usual. I got recently divorced, straight Danny Zuko to hug me more times than I'm sure he would have liked. I think he could tell I was feeling needy and sentimental. And I might have been imagining it, but he seemed to really hug me back tightly. At least that's what I convinced myself. The next morning I woke up in my tiny bedroom, and Zuzanna was already at class for the day, so I was all alone. I made some coffee, ate a newly expired yogurt that I had gotten on sale, and checked my service to see if I had any messages. I had one. My heart raced.

"Hey Andrew, this is Tiffany from *Rent* casting. Thank you for coming in last week. We are NOT going to need to see you again, we are going in a different direction this time, but you are definitely on the list for next time. Thanks, doll!"

That was it. I sat down on the sloppy daybed we used for a couch in our dirty living room. It was Monday morning, and all of a sudden I had no boyfriend, no job, and a filthy apartment. How had this all gone away so quickly? Couldn't I just have lost ONE of those things? Maybe two?

I got back into bed. I couldn't believe it, but I actually was having a moment of missing school, missing that schedule, and the safety of knowing I had someplace to be every day. I missed my friends from *Grease*. I missed Jim/Lyle and his stupid face and his tight singlet. I even missed the Westchester and its free buffet food. I was also feeling something else: anger at myself. I had let myself get distracted.

Yes, I was working as an actor, which was great, but I could have figured out a part-time job that would have alleviated a lot of my stress. Sure, Jim/Lyle was fun, but having sex with someone on Broadway is not the same as being on Broadway yourself. And worst of all, I had come to New York to learn how to be a better actor and I had dropped out of school with little thought. Money was a factor, but so was my ego. I had thought I was better than I was, that I somehow magically knew better than all my professors. I was not only angry with myself, but disappointed in myself. I had been living in New York City for two and a half years and I thought I knew my way around. Instead I found out I had just gotten myself lost.

Imaginary Omaha Andy

THERE WERE CERTAINLY SEVERAL MOMENTS IN MY first years in New York, weak moments, moments like the one at the end of the last chapter, when I wondered if I had made the right choice in moving there. Yes, it is where my soul felt most at home, but there were plenty of times when I wondered if my soul was a liar.

After leaving Marymount and moving in with Zuzanna, I really had to hustle to keep my head above water. I was mostly living on canned pineapple and tuna, my thought being that I could stave off scurvy and still get some protein. At twenty-one years old, I felt like I was too old to ask my parents for help. I had occasional acting jobs that would buoy my resolve, but there were many, many mornings when I would wake up on my twin mattress that did not have a frame and stare at the ceiling above me in my eight-by-ten-foot room. Hungry from skipping dinner the night before, with no auditions that day and no serious love life to speak of, I would torture/comfort myself by dreaming about what my life *could* have been like if I were still in Omaha . . .

I would have enrolled in UNO, the University of Nebraska in Omaha. It is a school that is sort of infamous for its high enrollment but low graduation rates. At a minimum it takes most people six or seven years to graduate. (This is an informal statistic that I have personally found to be true, not a state-issued fact.) I would have enrolled there, and I would have chosen "Communications" as my major. I wouldn't have known what "Communications" involved, but I think as a freshman I would have been intrigued enough to commit. I would have stayed at home, living with my parents for the first year to save more money. I would be going to class, learning how to communicate, and moonlighting as Omaha's Next Top Model, before coming home and watching *Home Improvement* or *Veronica's Closet* with my parents until I fell asleep.

The tricky piece of this puzzle would be my love life. I liked to think that I would have had the wherewithal to call it off for good with the forty-year-old, but I knew that at that age and in that headspace, I would have let it drag out for even longer. I for sure would have felt compelled to come out to my parents, and they would have had to deal with the fact that not only was I gay but I was also in a relationship with a forty-year-old man. This news would have created a bit of a rift between me and my parents, and I imagine the strain would have caused me to look for other housing. The obvious choice would have been to move in with the forty-year-old, which would have thrilled him and made me feel even more trapped. But I would have done it under the false pretense of independence.

Now living without my parents, but with another kind of parent, I would be at the mercy of panicked coupledom. Pieces of my life would start to slide into his, and I would start to lose focus at school. He would convince me to star in a local community theater production. I would acquiesce because I love to perform, but it would mean late nights out after rehearsals and skipping classes the next day. I would also start skipping class because of my local TV commercial career, since it was actually making me money. Before long I would stop going to my Communications classes altogether.

One community theater production would turn into three, and before too long I would be fully entrenched in the Omaha theater scene. My commercial career would be too erratic to count on, so I would have to get a day job, but something flexible. I would become a bartender at some popular Omaha restaurant, where I would run into high school classmates who were home for the holidays or summer break. They would ask, "Weren't you going to go to New York?"—and I would stammer and say, "I'm going next year. I'm just saving up some money first." We would both smile and know that was a lie, and then I would make them their Jack and Ginger.

I would go home to the forty-year-old's house and I would hate myself a little. I would hate him more. I would feel trapped and want to go to my parents', but because I was too proud, I would stay there and just twist myself into knots. There would be some good times though. I would enjoy performing in these local productions, even though there would be a nagging what-if pulling at my heart every time I took a bow. I would comfort myself by saying I was a big fish in this small pond and that was good enough for me. I would also get to play many great roles. Probably most of them I would be too young for, but I would still get cast because I was the hungriest. I would play a sprightly Bobby in *Company*, opposite costars who were all into their forties. I would play Nick in *Who's Afraid of Virginia Woolf?* but I would play it for laughs because I felt like it needed a lighter touch. I would play the most Gentile-looking Motel ever cast in *Fiddler on the Roof.* My performance calendar would be booked months in advance. I wouldn't be paid for any of these triumphs because it was community theater, so I would have to keep my bartending job, eventually getting angrier and angrier that I was the star of the show one night and cutting up cocktail fruit the next. I would be drinking a lot. I would be eating a lot. I would for sure have my tips frosted and be going to a tanning bed on a regular basis.

Years would go by too quickly. One morning, waking up hungover next to the now forty-five-year-old, whom I despised with all my heart, I would stumble to the bathroom and see myself in the mirror, my copper-y highlights askew and plastered to my head, making them seem even more haphazard and uneven. My fake tan would seem particularly orange in the bathroom light. I would see the marks under my eyes from the tanning goggles more clearly than usual. My body, now tens of pounds heavier from drink and processed foods, would disgust me. I would then start to surveil the room itself. The cheap burgundy bath towels folded fussily by the shower. The dream catcher in the window from our last vacation to Santa Fe. The Pumpkin Spice Yankee Candle by the sink. The poorly framed *Casablanca* poster hanging above the toilet. *My god, this guy has shitty taste,* I would think. But is this also *my* taste? Why am I living here? Why do I look like this? Why is this my life? Something would snap in my brain, like a fuse blowing or an ice cube cracking on your molars.

I've gotta get out of here.

I would grab a bag and shove what few belongings I actually liked inside, leaving behind several blazers from Structure and Nehru-collar shirts from J. Peterman. I would wake up the forty-year-old by shouting at him, "I'm leaving, fuck face! I'm out! I'm dead to you! Don't try to contact me ever again!" I would storm out of that house without letting him speak to me, and I would get in the Ford Escort that I had bought from my dad and drive straight to my parents' house. I would explain that I needed a place to stay to collect my thoughts and regroup. My parents would agree and not ask too many questions, which I would be grateful for. Over the next few months I would re-register for classes at UNO, now fully understanding what "Communications" meant. I would drop out of all community theater productions I had committed to and cut ties with most of the people I had interacted with.

I would let my tan fade and I would cut every last highlight out of my hair, starting fresh like a monk in an ashram. I would dig out my sister Julie's *Sweatin' to the Oldies* VHS tapes, and I would sweat to those oldies until I could fit back into the Abercrombie & Fitch chinos that I'd worn senior year of high school. I would throw myself into school, and being one of the oldest students in my class, I would stand out as a real force to be reckoned with. I would get an internship at KETV (our most popular local news source), and I would prove myself as a hard worker and dedicated student. I would probably have an affair with a local news anchor, because . . . Who am I kidding? I would have to make some mistakes somewhere. But it wouldn't be disruptive, and we would part ways maturely, without incident.

Most important, I would rebuild my relationship with my parents. I would make them proud and finally live up to the potential they had always seen in me.

Flash forward a couple years: I am now a full-blown anchor at KETV NewsWatch 7. I am known for my steady tone and empathic delivery, whether I am reporting on a State Fair Ferris wheel accident or the birth of a baby tiger at the Henry Doorly Zoo. People love me. I am respected. I live in a beautiful and tastefully decorated home in the Fairacres neighborhood of Omaha. I had to painstakingly restore every inch of original wood in the house, but you know what? It was worth it. A real labor of love. And I had the help of my wonderful boyfriend, Dr. Zack. Dr. Zack is a cardiologist at the Creighton University Medical Center. We met while he was taking care of my father after an irregular heartbeat was discovered. My dad actually suggested I meet Dr. Zack after he found out Dr. Zack was gay. Dr. Zack was a fan of mine after watching my six-part series about teen runaways living in the abandoned Southroads Mall. We hit it off and have been inseparable ever since. That was three years ago. We are seriously thinking about having a commitment ceremony in our backyard for our family and friends. You know? Something intimate. Just for us.

Yes, I really turned my life around in Omaha. It was looking iffy for a couple years there, but then I got it all sorted out. Do I ever miss performing? Oh, I don't know. Maybe sometimes. But I am quite fulfilled with my job now. I like helping people, telling their stories, connecting with the community. Would I ever think about a career in local politics? Me? Oh gosh, I mean, I'd be lying if I said I never thought about it. It's something Zack and I would have to talk about. We are considering starting a family. We've looked at adoptions in China and we are really close to ordering a toddler.

It's a big step, but I think we have a lot of love to give. We certainly have the space!

Eventually there would be holidays with the family at our house. Nieces and nephews playing in our yard. No nosey in-laws to deal with because Dr. Zack is, conveniently, an orphan. (But he's super well-adjusted about that.)

I would picture myself back in Omaha, living this *Sliding Doors* version of my life, and it all seemed right. It all seemed *perfect*. Too *perfect*. Too *safe*. At this point in my daydream I would usually hear a New York City police siren, or Zuzanna in the next room watching *Real World*, or my downstairs neighbor would start to blast "Crystal Blue Persuasion" at a deafening decibel, as he was wont to do. I would force myself to get out of bed, and I would think about the day ahead of me.

Anything was possible. I could do anything I wanted in New York City. Yes, I was poor. Yes, I was jobless. But I had everything to look forward to. I was here pursuing my dream, the dream I'd had since fourth grade. If Imaginary Omaha Andy could turn his life around and get what he wanted, so could Real Life New York Andrew. I didn't want to be a news anchor. I wanted to be on Broadway. I didn't want to restore an old mansion. I wanted to live in a co-op in Chelsea. I didn't want a kid from China. I wanted to be friends with Patti LuPone.

I would allow myself to have these daydream moments whenever I needed to, just to remind myself of what it was I was truly after, and while my alternate universe life was appealing, it always led me back to what it was I actually wanted.

I would still take a Dr. Zack though.

I Don't Want to Catch 'Em All

A HUGE FACTOR IN THE MENTAL INSTABILITY OF actors is the uncertainty of the business we have devoted our lives to. You can be nearly destitute one day, with no prospects, not even a glimmer of hope for success, and then with one phone call, the next months or even years of your life can completely change with a single job. You live with the power of possibility—and the burden of it— every day.

In the weeks following my final Hand Jive as Doody at the Westchester Broadway Theatre I found myself waking up and trying, desperately, to will the phone to ring with the news that would give my days a shape—and my life some purpose—once again. I didn't have an agent at the time, so the possibility of just magically getting a job on my own seemed bleak. I was not good at survival jobs, but it was becoming clear that if I didn't get another gig soon, I would have to dust off my skills as New York's most uncoordinated restaurant host or reprise my role as "Coatcheck Who Hides in the Bathroom." I reminded myself that I had booked work on my own before, and that I could do it again. I just wished that it would get easier at some point.

Miraculously, after months of what seemed like endless

rejections, I got a call from a casting director I had auditioned for a few months earlier for a non-Equity production of *Godspell*, a show that was always confusing to me. Why were they dressed as clowns? Why did the person playing Jesus have to wear a Superman T-shirt? Why was there a character named "Sonya"? Who the hell was she in the Bible? (I know it's the name of the original actress, Theater People, calm down.) I wasn't cast in *Godspell*, but I could tell that this casting director liked me. This time she said that she was casting a show at Radio City Music Hall that would run for a month of performances and then go on a brief tour across the country. It would be steady work for six months and the pay was $1,000 a week. I had never made that much money in my life. I hadn't even auditioned yet, but I was already mentally packing my bags and spending that paycheck. There was just one quick detail I thought I should go over before signing the contract: "What is the show?" I asked, not really caring what the answer would be.

"It's called *Pokémon Live!*"

I was taken aback. I had only a hazy understanding of what Pokémon was, or were. (Were they people? Animals?) My only reference point was the news story about the cartoon being so frenetic that it caused seizures in some children. The casting director sensed my immediate hesitation/ total fucking panic.

"You wouldn't be playing a Pokémon," she said. "You would be playing a human. The Pokémon are going to be puppets, I think."

Okay. This is looking a little bit better, I thought. *It's children's theater. I've done plenty of that, and this is at Radio City*

Music Hall for the love of God. This is just some highbrow children's theater. Then the casting director started telling me about the people involved in the show. The director was from the Broadway company of *Chicago*, the composer wrote all the music for the Pokémon TV show, and the book writer wrote on . . . wait for it . . . *Days of Our Lives*.

Let me explain something about how my head spun this information into me basically becoming Tom Hanks from my involvement in *Pokémon Live!* (The exclamation point was part of the title, by the way. It wasn't "Live" period, it was "LIVE" EXCLAMATION POINT, DAMN IT! These Pokémon were LIVING in front of your very eyes!) I heard "*Chicago*"—a show that happened to be wildly successful at the moment—and it immediately legitimized the entire operation. I wasn't totally sure how sexy Fosse dancers with bowler hats would work their way into *Pokémon Live!* but if I had my way, I would be brunching with Bebe Neuwirth in no time. Because the composer of this production worked on the Pokémon TV show, there would obviously be other TV people around, who, perhaps, would need my voice-over expertise at some point. And the book writer coming from *Days of Our Lives,* well . . . if he worked there, maybe he would see me and realize that I was perfect for soap opera work and whisk me away to Pine Valley or whatever fictional soap opera land *Days of Our Lives* takes place in. (I know it's Salem, Soap People, calm down.) I was already planning my next four moves after *Pokémon Live!* and I hadn't even gotten the job yet. I believe this shows a real ability to plan on my part and also a huge disconnect from reality. In any event, I was on board.

I showed up for the audition at Radio City Music Hall, which in and of itself was VERY exciting. I had never been to Radio City, so entering for the first time through the stage door was pretty frickin' cool. The hallways were plastered with posters of all the greats who had played there: James Taylor, Carole King, Stevie Wonder, the Rockettes, Jessica Simpson! The audition looked and felt like a normal audition. We sang, we danced a little, and then they started giving us scenes and pairing us up to read together.

The director was a handsome and intense man named Luis Perez. He had been in the original revival cast of *Chicago* but had recently left to pursue directing. I liked him immediately, and he seemed to know what he was doing. More important, he was more than a little eye roll-y about the whole project. When he was explaining what the show was about, there was a little wink accompanying all of it. He certainly didn't expect any of us to know the ins and outs of the Pokémon storylines.

The production team decided to have me read for both the male lead and the comedic villain, and both auditions seemed to go well. They asked a handful of us to come back later in the week, but this time we would need to learn some of the original music from the show. They gave us sheet music and a CD with the demo tracks, and we even had to sign nondisclosure agreements, which seemed silly. I mean, who the hell was I going to tell about this? But it also gave me the impression that these people weren't fucking around.

Luis also suggested that we watch the cartoon before we came back. "I don't want to see an impersonation, but you should just have a feel for the characters." *Research! I can do that!* I got on the subway and immediately put the CD in my Discman—it was 2000—so I could hear this secret music. I have to say, the songs weren't terrible. They were sort of benign pop songs with catchy hooks and vague lyrics, but they were fun. The songs all sort of sounded like Richard Marx had had a musical baby with Mandy Moore. I had to learn "The Time Has Come." (For what? I wasn't sure yet.) And "The Best at Being the Worst." (A possible premonition of my immediate future.) I was strangely excited about this callback. I could see that this show might be better than it seemed on paper.

I got back to my apartment, and it happened to be close to the time *Pokémon* was going to be on television. It was a big after-school hit, and I think they ran two episodes in a row, so I could really dive into my research. I turned on the show, ready to break down the psychological intricacies of each Pokémon character. Now, I don't know if you have ever seen *Pokémon*, but it looks and sounds like a combination of the worst fever dream you have ever had mixed with the volume and intensity of a grade school playground street fight. Everyone on the show was screaming their lines and seemed incredibly angry or scared. Or both.

The actual Pokémon characters were these odd-looking, colorful creatures who could only communicate by saying their names. For example, there was a turtle-like thing whose name was "Squirtle." (I didn't make that up, that is a character's name and not an autofill response on a YouPorn search page.) "Squirtle" would just say his name over and over again, and the other characters would somehow understand what he was trying to tell them. A typical scene might look like this:

HUMAN PERSON
Come on, Squirtle, what's wrong?

SQUIRTLE
Squirtle squirtle squirtle squirtle squirtle.

HUMAN PERSON
I know you don't want to go home, but we have to.

SQUIRTLE
Squirtle squirtle.

HUMAN PERSON
Thanks for understanding, buddy.

SQUIRTLE
Squirtle.

END OF SCENE

I was really struggling to get through this episode and not have some kind of aneurysm. I could see why children were having seizures while watching this show. I muted the sound and decided to just wait for the characters I was auditioning for to come on screen. Helpfully, in the demo CD, there were pictures of the characters for reference. My characters' names were Ash and James, the latter being part of a villainous duo named Team Rocket. I was less interested in the villain and more interested in Ash. His song was better and he was the lead. If I was going to whore it out for children's theater, I might as well be the lead, right? I finally saw Ash on TV and turned up the sound. It was clearly a woman who was voicing this character. She had a raspy voice and stayed true to the line-reading screamfest that was already established. Rather than sounding like a teenage boy, she sounded more like an angry office manager who smoked a couple packs a day. I wasn't sure if I could accurately do this voice, but I remember Luis telling us he didn't want an impression. Maybe there was some room for reinterpretation.

In the same scene, my other character, James, and his partner in crime, Jessie, appeared. I was shocked to see that James had purple, bob-length hair and even more shocked to hear his voice. It was basically the most offensive impression of a gay man you could possibly do without putting a cartoon dick in the character's mouth at all times. I was horrified and offended for my people. How was this on television? How was this acceptable for children to watch? I decided that I would focus on Ash and leave the other character for some other actor with less self-esteem to tackle.

As I sat in my room, working on this material, I was bounced between genuine excitement about the project's potential and total terror that I might actually get this job and have to do it. But I had no other viable options. *I don't have the job yet*, I told myself. *Let's take this one step at a time.*

I went to my callback ready to nail my Ash audition. I was just going to tell the casting director that I couldn't read for the role of James, that I simply wasn't comfortable with the material. Surely she would respect my integrity. So when the time came, I marched up to her and, in the most positive way possible, told her that I wasn't "feeling" the role of James and that I just wanted to read Ash. She frowned at me a little. "What's wrong?" she asked while tilting her head to the side in a way that felt pretty aggressively passive-aggressive.

"Nothing is wrong, I am just relating to the lead, I mean Ash, more. I hope that's okay."

Her head somehow tilted even more. I'm not sure how it was staying on her body.

"But you would be so funny, Andrew! I know that the whole team is really excited to see what you do with that part."

I'm embarrassed to say that even that tiny little compliment, or suggestion of a compliment, was enough to throw me off my integrity wagon.

"Can I be honest?" I said to her, now mimicking her head tilt. "I thought the voice was a little offensive. It was so over-the-top."

"Oh my god! Totally! I totally feel that. But you don't have to do that voice. You don't have to do that at all. Luis really wants everyone to make this *their own*." There's that fucking phrase that tricks actors time and time again. Anytime someone tells you to "make it your own" what they really mean is "read my mind and figure out what I can't articulate." But at the time I thought maybe it indeed meant "make it your own," so I folded and said that I would read the role of James and really try to put my own spin on it.

I read and sang all my Ash material first. It went well. Better than well. It was great. I sang the hell out of it. I think the reading was appropriately cheesy and earnest, and the whole team seemed happy, excited even. Then I had a little break while they read other parts, so I had a moment to work on this James material. As I read it and reread it, I could see where there was some room to get away from the "Hollywood" from *Mannequin* stereotype. I could make this funny without getting myself blacklisted by GLAAD. I was feeling better about it, but I still wanted that other part.

At this point, because James was part of a duo, they paired us up and asked us to read with a partner. Mine was a very small, very beautiful young woman named Lauren Kling. She was probably a foot shorter than I was but made up for it with her hair, which was all blown out, teased, and piled on her head in a sloppy but sexy updo. She looked like she had just had sex in the back of a car after prom—in the best possible way. We read the scene together and we got laughs; we just sort of clicked. After we read, Luis told us how great we were, and then he asked me, "Andrew, you've seen the cartoon, right?" I knew exactly where this was going, but I couldn't stop it.

"Yes, I have."

"Great. So you know James has a pretty specific way of talking, right?"

You mean like that old queen on I Love Lucy who keeps saying, "Well, Mrs. RIIIICAAAARRRDOOOO!"

"Yes, I think I know what you mean."

"Do you think you could do it again with more of that in there?"

You mean sell myself and my people down the river and act like Longtime Companion *or* The Normal Heart *never happened? Like Stonewall wasn't a thing? Like Harvey Milk didn't exist?*

"Sure, I can do that."

We read the scene again, and I made a split-second decision to just give them what they wanted. They wanted "Just Jack" penetrating Liberace, and I was going to give it to them.

I regretted it the second we started, but the gay train had left the offensive ass station. The worst part of all was that I was really good at it. The room was doubled over in laughter and applauded when we finished. Lauren looked at me as we walked out of the room, "Well, we booked this gig," she said.

And she was right. We got called the next day with all the information about dates and money and contracts. The thing about getting a yes after getting ninety-nine nos is that it is exciting. It's a win. It might not be exactly the win you wanted, but it's still a win. It's like when you get a $5 prize on a $1,000 scratch ticket. You're not a total loser. And I was straight-up financially destitute at this point. This was a big win wrapped in a potentially embarrassing bow.

A week or so later, I was rehearsing at Radio City Music Hall every day. Walking through that stage door in the morning never got old. I felt fancy, fancier than I deserved to feel given the project. But Luis and his team really worked hard to make us feel like we were telling a story and playing real people instead of cartoons. As far as I can recall, the plot of *Pokémon Live!* went like this: Our hero, Ash, and his friends, Misty and Brock, have to go searching for Ash's missing Pokèmon and best friend, Pikachu. Still with me? Pikachu has been captured by a villain named Giovanni and his two hilarious henchpeople, Jessie and James. (That's where I enter.) There's action and laughs and lots of singing and dancing. The emotional stakes were high, my friends. Life or death for little Pikachu!

The cast, myself included, all started to drink the Pokèmon Kool-Aid. When you are in rehearsal with no audience, you start to lose track of what's actually funny or good. You make one another laugh, you build one another up, and it's all necessary to create a show. The Broadway director Jack O'Brien calls them "Equity Laughs." But usually you are in for a bit of a rude awakening when you get in front of your first audience. It's like trying at dinner to explain to your spouse something hilarious that happened at work. It usually doesn't land. He doesn't know who Karen from accounting is. It's not funny that she fell in the Xerox room. He finds that story sad.

Our rude awakening happened a little sooner. Throughout the rehearsal process, we had been rehearsing in our cute workout clothes, looking very much like ourselves. Then came the day that reality appeared and smacked us all in the face: our final costume fittings. My smack came in the form of a purple bob-length wig and a white jumpsuit. I remember looking in the mirror and thinking, *I can't go through with this. I cannot be seen on stage in this costume.* But it was too late for that. I was in too deep. And to be fair, no one had been spared. The entire cast looked like assholes.

The one consolation was that *Pokémon Live!* was actually well received. The show was nearly sold out at Radio City for every performance—a testament to the popularity of Pokémon—and our time performing there flew by, particularly because the schedule was so brutal. We did four shows a day, most days, which meant we never got out of costume. We just toweled off the sweat, reapplied our makeup, and did another show. It was tough. But six thousand enthusiastic kids in the audience made it easier.

The real struggles began when we hit the road for our mini-tour. We were playing both Broadway touring houses and huge arenas usually reserved for sporting events or major concerts. When we would get to these venues, we would often play to houses that were only a third full. It was still a lot of people, but three thousand people in a nine-thousand-seat arena looks very sad. And we were generally so far away from the audience that we couldn't hear if they even existed.

We never knew what to expect when we arrived in a new city. We played either Broadway touring houses or huge concert venues. I remember one day in particular, we were performing at the Indianapolis State Fair Coliseum, which was used for concerts, and also for the Ice Capades and Junior NHL games. (That's hockey for you non-sports folks.) This meant that the floor of the arena was made of ice, and when shows such as ours came through, they would lay plywood boards over the ice and set up seating on top for the audience. Backstage, however, they did not lay plywood over the ice. Instead, they just created pathways so that the cast could get to the stage without slipping. It was cold and treacherous to walk off the strict path we were given. I saw more than my share of castmates bite it on that ice because they didn't listen. Not this guy though! I value my coccyx!

One night, I remember sitting on top of a storage crate with one of my castmates, Heidi. She was wearing a truly unfortunate orange wig styled into a high side ponytail, a crop top, Daisy Duke shorts, and suspenders. I was in my full James drag, and we were huddled together, wrapped in a blanket. We sat in silence for a long time, listening to the sound of *Pokémon Live!* play out on stage for the two hundredth time. And without saying a word to each other, we just started crying. Just like my summer at the Theater Barn,

I suddenly felt so far away from New York. From Zuzanna and our evenings out. From the life I had managed to create for myself there. There was nothing to do at that moment but cry. And drink.

We boozed it up like idiots on that tour. We would finish our show and then just hit it hard almost every night. We were young, we had enough money to make us dangerous, and we were bored. We would shut down the bar at every hotel we were staying in, and then continue the party in our hotel rooms, much to the horror and annoyance of the other guests. I'm not proud to say this, but I will admit it, *Pokémon Live!* was the first time I experienced a blackout from drinking. If you have never experienced a blackout, it's not something I recommend. You literally lose time in a way that is very disorienting the next morning. It's strange to think that the period of time I was trying to black out was my time on stage and that the time I actually blacked out was my free time.

And look, it wasn't all terrible. I was working with great people—really kind, fun people—and I was grateful for the job. I'm still grateful for that job. It kept me afloat for a long time and led to some really great opportunities after the show closed. I never got to have brunch with Bebe Neuwirth, nor was I cast on *Days of Our Lives*, but I did end up doing a lot of voice-over work. However . . . the daily humiliation of playing that part, in that costume—knowing that I was selling myself short and playing a gay clown for the amusement of everyone in America—was hard. Harder than I was willing to admit. There's a fear as a gay actor that once you play a gay part, or in this case, the cartoon depiction of a gay part, you will be typecast in that role forever. And while the stakes were low on this particular production and no one knew who the hell I was, I was young enough to worry that maybe playing one-dimensional gay characters was going to be my future. Plus, I felt like I was doing a disservice to any gay kid who saw that show and thought that's how we had to behave. Like we had to play the fool, be the punchline.

The whole thing made me sad. But I learned an important lesson during *Pokémon Live!*: I wasn't going to put myself in that position again. I was going to be better about saving my money so that I didn't have to take a job I didn't want in order to survive. I also wasn't going to demean myself or the gay community just to get a laugh. I would gladly play gay parts, but the laughs would be on my terms. In reality, I wouldn't play another gay role for over ten years, when I was cast on *Girls*, but I certainly turned down a lot of auditions for stuff that didn't sit well with me. We all have our line, and I learned where mine was early in my career, and I am grateful for that. There would be no more gay clowning, no more compromising my self-esteem, and no more purple bob wigs.

By the way, I still can't tell you what the fuck Pokémon is about.

Party Monsters

As we said good-bye to our teens and embraced our twenties in the city, Zuzanna and I made the bold choice to party like we were already well into our fifties. When we weren't closing Rose's Turn or processing a bizarre show at Stingy Lulu's, we liked to sit and drink wine for long stretches of time while talking about movies or books or things happening in New York. When we ran out of those things to discuss, we would land on our favorite topic: ourselves. But even narcissism has its limits. Eventually we would get bored with ourselves and go out into the world and act our age. We were in New York City, and if *200 Cigarettes* had taught us anything, it was that there were experiences to be explored and adventures to be had. We would sensibly research "clubs" and see where the cool people were going.

We tried Tunnel. It was very crowded and very loud. Zuzanna and I ended up getting locked in a cage with strangers for what seemed like an hour and were forced to dance until someone let us out. I think it was supposed to be an honor to be locked in the cage, but it didn't feel like one. Instead it felt like . . . well, it felt like we were *locked in a cage*.

Next up was Twilo. It turns out the night we went to Twilo, everyone was at Tunnel.

There was the second incarnation of the Limelight. It was mostly gay men, which was fun for me but less fun for Zuzanna. We ended up just walking around and shouting at each other, "It's so weird this used to be a church!" The weirdest part was that it still looked like a church. It's like if all of a sudden Our Lady of Lourdes in Omaha started hosting raves after midnight mass. It was excitingly sacrilegious.

We attempted to roller-skate at the Roxy. Zuzanna had grown up ice-skating, but it turns out ice-skating and roller-skating require two very different skill sets. And I was rusty from the days of grade school skating parties at Skateland in Omaha. We managed not to break anything or majorly embarrass ourselves, but ultimately we didn't last long.

We went to a big, sloppy party at the Bowery Bar. It was mostly filled with young, douchey finance guys and girls who looked like they worked in advertising. A lot of Brians and Ashleys. I accidentally put my cigarette out on a man as we were trying to make our way to the bar. After some shouting and sweaty apologizing, we figured we should probably leave the premises before we were asked to.

To try something a little further afield, Zuzanna took me to a hip-hop club in Harlem one night. She was very popular there, I was not. Although a number of people thought I was Ryan Reynolds circa *Two Guys, a Girl and a Pizza Place*, so that was fun for me.

And then there was the night I dragged her to the Cock in the East Village. She had in town from Indiana a high school friend who had just recently come out. I thought taking him to the most aggressive gay bar in the city might be fun for him. He ended up getting his wallet stolen while getting a blow job in the back room. But at least he got a blow job.

We would attempt these excursions a couple times a month with varying degrees of success. We would put on our "clubbing looks," which were mostly mismatched, all-black outfits that were either too tight or too big. We'd venture out to brave lines, excessively loud music, and $10 vodka sodas (which were outrageous at the time and in my mind still are). We'd force ourselves to dance about until finally one of us would look at the other and say, "Are you ready to go?" Then we would go find a pizza place or a diner and wrap up our evening with a heavy bedtime snack and one of those long conversations about life that you only seem to have in your twenties. Finding the right club for us was starting to feel a lot like dating. We just weren't meeting the right ones. We needed a new strategy.

One day Zuzanna came home from school and told me about a hot new party she'd heard about. It was at a club called Mother in the Meatpacking District, which at this point was not what it is today. It was certainly better than it had been in the seventies, but there wasn't a Stella McCartney store or a Dylan's Candy Bar yet. It was still a neighborhood that processed meat during the day and got awfully quiet at night, with the exception of prostitutes and drug dealers. It seemed dangerous, like one of the few neighborhoods in Manhattan untouched by gentrification.

Once a month Mother hosted a "fetish night," and Zuzanna had heard that it was a lot of fun. It seemed unexpected and weird and incredibly different from our mainstream club outings. Maybe that was what was missing. Maybe we just needed a Fetish Night! It was there that we ran into our first problem: What was our fetish? The postcard advertising the party said, "Leather, Rubber, and All Kinks." Did we have a kink? Could I get into rubber? We needed help planning this outing.

A couple years after I moved to New York, a childhood friend of mine, Randi—the one who also happened to be my prom date two years in a row—moved to New York, too. When we were kids she was the most beautiful, most talented person at the Emmy Gifford Children's Theater. She was funny and clever and she sang with vibrato, which put her light-years ahead of the rest of us. She also had an aggressive naiveté about her sex appeal that was shocking to adults but impressive to her peers. Adults at the theater used to call her "Lolita" behind her back. We would hear this and, not fully understanding what it meant, assume it was a compliment.

Since I'd moved to New York, I'd sort of lost track of her, and then one year she magically appeared in Manhattan as if she had belonged there all along. She'd had some rather colorful jobs since I'd last seen her, including lingerie model and phone sex operator, and while she was rather new to the city, I knew that she'd be able to help us figure out our "kinks." Randi wisely suggested we head to the East Village and shop the stores on St. Marks Place for inspiration. We marched into Trash and Vaudeville at St. Marks and Second Avenue ready to get our kink on. We all immediately found costumes—or just *clothes* depending on how you live your life, no judgments here—but it turns out that my love for leather jumpsuits reaches its limit at six hundred bucks. We had to come up with a plan that wouldn't cost us all of our savings accounts.

We decided that we could just find suggestive T-shirts and go from there. Fetishes are about attitude, we decided based on nothing, so we would just internalize our fetishes and live them for all to see. Zuzanna found a tight black shirt with a zipper cutting across the bust line that showed off her cleavage. The effect was truly obscene and exactly what she was looking for. I found an even smaller T-shirt that had the words HOOKER 2000 printed across the front in bright pink letters. I figured that looking like a twink-y rent boy would probably suffice. I also bought a pair of fashion glasses just for good measure. I guess I thought I would be a bookish twink-y rent boy? I don't know. Randi didn't buy anything and we didn't question her. She seemed way ahead of us already as usual.

The night of our big Mother outing came, and we all changed into our looks as we slammed glass after glass of the cheapest white wine we could find in the largest bottle possible. (Thanks, Cavit Pinot Grigio and the folks at Town Wine and Spirits who never carded me!) I tried to make my hair as River Phoenix–like as my Murray's Pomade would allow, and Zuzanna put hers in pigtails, which seemed correct. Randi just applied more eyeliner and removed her bra from under her tiny tank top. We were ready to go!

We didn't trust ourselves to find Mother on foot since we weren't familiar with the Meatpacking District and we didn't want to get mugged before getting to at least dance a little. Also our looks didn't seem subway-appropriate, so we decided to splurge on a cab. We pulled up to Mother, and there was only a small line outside. (I should mention that we never nailed "timing" on any of these outings. If the party started at 11 p.m., we would arrive at 11:30 p.m., thinking that a half hour was probably enough time for things to really get going. The rest of the club would arrive at 2 a.m., usually when Zuzanna and I had had enough. We *never* learned our lesson.)

The bar was sparsely populated when we entered, giving us a chance to acclimate ourselves to the environment. (In other words, to keep drinking until we felt comfortable.) If we were self-conscious about our looks on the street, those fears quickly went away once other patrons arrived. There were people on leashes, people with ball gags in their mouths, men in leather gimp suits, French maids, men dressed as biker cops, a man tied to a rack with a woman in stilettos standing on top of him. The scene only got crazier as the bar got more crowded. The music was fun, but no one was really dancing. It was more a "stand around and look at people" kind of vibe, which was fine by us.

As time often passes in clubs like this, all of a sudden hours had gone by and we were now packed in the center of the room, surrounded by people who really knew what Fetish Night was all about. Randi nudged me and pointed to a woman dressed as Lieutenant Uhura from *Star Trek*. "That looks like Debbie Harry," Randi said. I am and have been a Debbie Harry and Blondie fan since I was a tiny child. After seeing them perform "Rapture" on *Solid Gold*, I asked my parents if we could buy the album. They did me one better and bought me the 8-track. (The Rannells family was never really on the cutting edge of technology. My mother still to this day owns a TV with a VHS player in it.) My dad thought my undying love for Debbie Harry was hilarious, I think hoping that I had a crush on her. The reality was, I wanted to BE her. Up to this point in my life, I had never seen Debbie in person and I would have gladly removed a rib to do so. I stared at Lieutenant Uhura.

"That's not her," I said. "There's no way."

"That is definitely her," Randi replied.

Between the beehive wig she was wearing, the lighting of the club, and the smoke from the, well, smokers, I couldn't really be sure. I decided the only thing to do was to ask. Emboldened by drink, I marched over to Lieutenant Uhura ready to disprove Randi's theory. I got dangerously close to her face and discovered . . . it was fucking Debbie Harry. "Rapture"! "Call Me"! Velma Von Tussle! It was her! I was not prepared for this. What could I say? What could I say to this *icon*? I managed to string together the following sentence: "Miss Harry, I love you. *Autoamerican* was the first 8-track I ever owned."

She stared at me for a moment. She took in my outfit. And then she smiled and said, "Thanks. I like your shirt." As she said it, she ran her hand down my chest, across the lettering of HOOKER 2000.

I wanted to say more, I wanted to make her love me back, but I also knew it would never get better than what had just happened. I had met an idol, she was dressed as a *Star Trek* character, and I was dressed as a twink hooker. I got to profess my love for her, and she said she liked my shirt while touching me. *Get out, Rannells!* I thought. *Get out before you ruin it!* With that, I said, "Thank you," to Ms. Debbie Harry and I walked away proudly.

When I got back to Randi, she said, "It wasn't her, right?"

"It was her. And she likes my shirt" was all I could say.

By this point in the evening, Randi and I were drunk and

losing our voices from screaming above the music as we tried to talk to people. We found Zuzanna chatting up a gentleman tied to a pole with nylon ropes. We decided it was time to go.

Once out of the club, we automatically headed to where most evenings ended, an all-night diner near Zuzanna's and my apartment to eat various fried foods and recap our adventure. That was always the best part of any night anyway, the conversations after we escaped the noise of the clubs. We could tell hilarious stories over mozzarella sticks and tuna melts, and then unabashedly talk about our goals without being self-conscious. We could make fun of each other's choices in men, and then, somehow, share our deepest fears about failing, without fear of judgment. We could just listen and cheerlead, and then order more Diet Cokes and do it all over again. Looking back, I think those were the nights when Zuzanna and I really forged our friendship. We might not have been *club people*, but we were adventurous and ambitious on our own terms, and that was okay with us.

I kept that HOOKER 2000 shirt for several more years, for the record. I mean, Debbie Harry touched it. I couldn't just throw it away.

My Second Date with Brad

I DON'T REMEMBER HIS LAST NAME. IF I DID SOME sort of deep dive into my psyche and really rooted around in there, I'm sure it would come back to me. But why? What would the point of that be? His first name was Brad, which is the perfect name for a relatively faceless memory from your early twenties. He was handsome, he had a nice smile, and he had startlingly blue eyes. I had always thought that when the eyes got too blue it looked like a person didn't have a soul. You are seeing too deeply into their head, and there's nothing back there. But I had never dated anyone with blue eyes, and it was springtime. All seemed okay in that moment. He also had a very nice body—fit, muscle-y, extremely soft skin.

The sex was good, I think. It was blow-job sex, if I recall correctly. There is a great debate among straight women and gay men as to what counts as "sex." I count it all. If someone has an orgasm, I count it. My female friends have a deep misunderstanding that for gay men, anal sex is like a handshake. I got news, ladies. Sometimes we don't want to do it with our dates as much as you don't want to do it with yours.

Plus, this was only a second date with Brad. We didn't know each other that well. We never would. The other detail I should share is that he wore a lot of Acqua di Giò. If you were sexually active in the early two thousands, you know exactly what that smell is. Much like its predecessor, CK One, it can trigger all sorts of sexual and romantic memories for a generation of adults. His haircut was a little fussy, his hands were a little feminine, but his fragrance was attractive.

An added bonus, he lived blocks away from me in Astoria, and if you have ever lived in Astoria, you know that sometimes getting people to go there at the end of the night is like asking a stranger for a ride to the airport. Brad was going to do for now. I was dating and I was twenty-two and independent and I had highlights.

The conversation at dinner was dull, but he laughed at almost everything I said, so for a comedy narcissist like me, he was an ideal dinner companion. As we ate, my Nokia flip phone started ringing. It was my sister Julie. I declined the call. My phone was less than a year old and I was still getting used to it. I didn't love that people could now reach me whenever they wanted. I liked my answering service better. I liked having to call in and get my messages. It made me feel like Rock Hudson or Doris Day. My father started showing me the movies of Betty Grable at a young age, and she was always checking her service for messages from suitors or Hollywood producers. There was a faded glamour to a service number.

After dinner, we went to a cheap Thai place packed with other gays on dates, and then decided to get a drink at a gay bar where, once again, we were surrounded by other gays on dates. Because what's more fun than trying to not look like you are checking other people out while learning about your date's siblings? So Brad and I drank our Cosmos (it was 2001, people; if Carrie Bradshaw was doing it, so was I) until his eyes began to look less soulless in the disco lights and we started kissing. (He was a very good kisser. Or my bar was low. It doesn't matter.) My phone vibrated again. Different sister. Becky this time. I ignored it. Another round, more making out, another phone call, Julie again. My level of drunkenness, mixed with my desire to be "present" for Brad, made this series of phone calls easy to dismiss. I had just finished reading *The Four Agreements*—Oprah recommended it—and I was really nailing "Be impeccable with your word." I had told Brad we were going on a date, and I was going to be ON this date, damn it. The making out started to turn a corner, meaning we were lying down on a banquette, and I had just enough sense left to suggest a cab.

I was feeling like a high roller, so I offered to pay. More important, even at twenty-two I was sensitive to bad lighting, and the MTA flattered no one. I don't remember the cab ride. I think there was more groping, more kissing, more picturing him as Paul Walker. We got to my apartment and we went straight to the bedroom. It lasted longer than it needed to. It was that new, "look how long I can last" phase. And then there was the cuddling and holding and sweating and panic and the kind of falling asleep next to a basic stranger and then waking up and thinking *Do I like this? Does he like this?* Before I knew it, almost two hours had passed.

I gently excused myself to use the bathroom, and while up I decided to look at my phone again. Six more missed calls. My stomach dropped. I was sober enough now to know that something was clearly wrong. I started listening to the messages. Julie was in hysterics from the first word. Something about my dad falling and an ambulance, I could barely make it out. Next message, Becky was calmer but sounded shaken. A heart attack or a stroke; they weren't sure. He was in an ambulance. Next: My mom telling me not to panic. Next: Julie, telling me it was time to panic. I skipped ahead. The last call was from my brother-in-law, Doug, and it was from only fifteen minutes earlier. I called his number. He answered. I didn't know my brother-in-law super-well at the time. He immediately started crying on the phone. I knew whatever had happened that night was bad. Doug explained that during my niece's first birthday party—I had completely forgotten it was her birthday even though I was her god-father—my dad had collapsed moments after handing off the hamburgers he'd been grilling.

The party was at my parents' house, though at this mo-ment my dad wasn't living there. My parents were in the pro-cess of getting a divorce. My first summer away from home, I'd read a book called *Beachcombing at Miramar*, which I now understand was a memoir of a man who was having a midlife crisis. He abandoned all responsibility and restarted his life on a beach in Northern California. I was struggling with the decision of whether or not to stay in college, and I was able to reinterpret this story to fit my needs, using it as backup to support my decision to ultimately drop out. I'd suggested my mother read it, I guess to tip her off that I might be leaving school, but it turned out she was able to reinterpret the same story to fit her needs and support her decision to leave my father. (I know this book is not the reason my parents split up, but the timing is suspect.)

My father, at sixty-one, had moved into a truly depressing bachelor pad near his office. The last time I'd been home, which had been about a month before this night, my youngest sister, Natalie, and I had visited him in his new place. The walls were beige and so was the carpet. The furniture my dad had picked out was all too large and dark for the space. It was filled with stuff and yet somehow still looked empty. He was trying to make it a home, but he didn't know how.

I immediately went into his bathroom to cry. I didn't want him to see me feeling sorry for him, but when I saw him in that space, my heart broke. He didn't belong there, he belonged in his home. I pulled myself together and the three of us ate sandwiches and Pringles. When he opened his kitchen cupboard, I saw that it was stocked with canned stews, probably the only thing he could successfully make in an indoor kitchen. I had to clench my jaw tightly to keep from crying again.

After dinner, my dad told Natalie and me that he wanted us to feel at home in his new place. I suggested I stay there the next time I came to visit. He seemed happy when I said that. Natalie and I left his apartment, both feeling depressed but trying to appear cheerful. I hope we did a good job. As we exited, my dad was standing at the top of the stairs, and I turned around and I yelled up the stairs, "I love you, Dad." And he replied, "I love you, Andy." It was the last thing I said to him.

Now I was listening to Doug cry and tell me about my dad's collapse. How he'd tried to do CPR, how the paramedics had used the paddles twice to get a weak pulse, how they'd whisked him away to the hospital, where he was now in a coma.

I imagined the scene: the birthday party decorations, the toys in the yard, the deck where he fell, the pots of plants my mom put out every spring, my mom crying, my sisters and brother crying, the uneaten hamburgers, the little girl's birthday cake. It was all too much. I started to cry loudly.

Brad came out to see what was wrong. At first I couldn't look at him, but then I finally did. His hair was mussed from half sleep and he was completely nude. He came and stood in front of me, his penis (which was strangely semi-erect) at eye level.

I tried to get more information from Doug. What hospital was my dad in? Where was my mom? Should I get on a plane tonight? I gestured for Brad to sit down. He sat close to me and started rubbing my back. It felt like torture. I was embarrassed about crying in front of Brad, but I also didn't care enough to stop. Doug talked me through what little information he had and suggested I call one of my sisters. I didn't know what to say. I imagined how horribly he must have felt kneeling over my father, trying to get his heart to beat, surrounded by people crying and shouting. All I could manage was "*Thank you.*" And then I hung up.

Brad tried to hug me. I felt his dick on my leg. My body went stiff. "What happened?" he asked. I managed my rage and my desire to shout, "Clearly nothing good, asshole! Put on some fucking pants!" I tried to explain to Brad in as few words as possible what had happened. He was asking a lot of questions that I didn't have the answers for. He started pacing around the apartment, still fully naked, making suggestions as to what I should do now. I stopped Brad as calmly as I could. My tears had completely dried up and been replaced with disgust for the whole situation.

I didn't even like this guy. Why did I have sex with him?

All of a sudden, everything seemed wrong. The apartment I was staying in seemed cramped and dirty and I hated everything inside of it. I caught myself in the mirror and I cringed at my dyed blond hair. Why did I do that? I looked like a fool.

I felt dirty and embarrassed, and most of all I just wanted to be alone. I told Brad he should go, that I needed to make some phone calls. He came and sat next to me again and put his arm around me. "You shouldn't be alone right now." He kissed my cheek. I leaned into him for a moment. I didn't want to be alone. I didn't want to be where I was. Everything was off and I felt so uncomfortable in my body. Is this what my dad felt like in that weird, sad apartment he was living in? Did he just feel off all the time? I kissed Brad lightly on the lips. "I really need you to leave right now," I said. He seemed hurt, which made me angry. And sad. We stood up. He hugged me for way too long. I felt his dick against me, through my sweatpants. "Okay!" I said. "Good-bye!" I walked into the bathroom and locked the door. I stared out the window listening to him get dressed. Then I heard the front door shut. He was finally gone.

The next few hours were filled with activity and confusion that finally ended with me back in Omaha for my dad's funeral. I rarely thought of Brad again. There were a few text messages from him that I never responded to. A voicemail some weeks later that also went unanswered. There was too much to sort through in the following months. And I was embarrassed, I suppose.

About two years later, Brad walked past me on Ninth Avenue. We almost stopped but only nodded at each other, smiled awkwardly, and kept going. I felt like I owed him some explanation, some ending to our story, but I just couldn't do it. I had to keep moving forward.

I had straightened out much of what felt so wrong that night. I now had a job I was proud of, an apartment I was proud of. I had buried my father and in doing so buried that whole chapter of my life. That meant that there could be no Brad, no trace of that time, of that night. I know it's not generous or kind, but that's what I did. Most important, I never got highlights again.

Our Good-bye to Ron

WHEN I GOT ON THAT PLANE TO HEAD HOME TO Omaha, I was still pretending to be optimistic. My dad was not dead yet. Even though Ron Rannells was a "Do Not Resuscitate" kind of guy, in the chaos of his collapse at a one-year-old's birthday party, the paramedics had hooked him up to a whole host of machines that were keeping him alive. *He might wake up*, I kept telling myself. *He could be fine.* But I had also packed the one black suit I owned, because I knew in my heart that I would be attending a funeral. I remember making small talk with the flight attendants on that flight. They had no idea why I was on the plane, and I wasn't about to tell them. I wanted to pretend for a while that everything was fine.

It wouldn't be fine. My family knew that Ron would not want to be kept alive by machines. At least he wouldn't be in pain, and it would be over quickly—or so I thought. I had falsely assumed, I guess because of movies and television, that the moment life support was turned off, the patient immediately died. This is not the case. Or at least it wasn't with my dad. We were told by doctors that it could be hours, maybe even days, before his heart once again stopped beating on its own. I stayed in the room with my mom as the machines were shut down. I wanted to be there, for him and for her.

We sat in silence for a long time. The nurses, after taking out all the various tubes and monitors attached to Ron, had combed his hair and straightened his hospital gown. He looked like himself again. It was much sadder than I had prepared myself for. I don't know why, but all of a sudden I felt compelled to ask my mom about her father's death. She told me he had also suffered from a heart attack, and had died, in a hospital room just like this, a month after I was born. As my mother talked about that last day with him, I felt my throat tighten, my face flush. I suddenly felt terrible that I had never asked my mother about her own father dying.

Two days later, with only my mother in the room, Ron passed away quietly.

Now began the business of planning Ron's funeral. We hadn't talked about many details, I suppose because we all hoped we wouldn't have to. I was not a stranger to funerals. Not only did I come from a large family with relatives who always seemed to be passing away, my stint as an altar boy meant that I had started serving funerals at eleven years old. I got to see all of it up close: the body in the casket, the grieving families, the funerals where hundreds of people came, the funerals where maybe ten people came. I was fascinated. I started to notice the details of each service: what made a good one, what made a bad one, what I would have done differently. My theatrical sensibilities mixed with my love of party planning (even as a child) went into full effect. Funerals were dramatic. The stakes were high for everyone involved.

Though I'd had a front row seat for many funerals, I had never actually planned one before. Now here I was, at twenty-two, looking at caskets for my father with my mother and my siblings. My parents were separated at the time he died but technically still married, which put my mother in an uncomfortable position. She was being treated like the grieving widow, which she was, but she was also not on good terms with our father when he died. I remember her pulling back a bit while we made these funeral decisions, maybe out of respect for us or just because of the awkwardness of the situation.

I struggled with my feelings for my mom at this time. I felt bad for her—she had just lost her husband of thirty-three years—but I also partially blamed her for his death. I mean, his heart problems were really the fault of red meat and Pepsi-Cola products, but she broke his heart when it was already weak.

I can't speak for my siblings, but for me, there were too many feelings to be felt at this time. Too many emotional land mines at every turn. I couldn't navigate them all, I didn't want to. So I did what seemed to be the most responsible thing to do at that time: denied all my feelings and distracted myself with humor.

At times like this, I'm glad that the Rannells family has a way of lightening the mood when most needed. It's in our blood. So it wasn't really a surprise when we all started making inappropriate jokes throughout the funeral preparation process. All of my siblings are funny, but my youngest sister, Natalie, is our MVP of Inappropriateness. Here are some of her best one-liners from the days surrounding our dad's death.

When our dad was still on life support and lying in his ICU bed:

NATALIE
Hey, Dad. It's Natalie. I got my period today.

MOM
Natalie!

NATALIE
What? I thought it might shock him out of it!

When we were signing the papers to take our father off life support and his handsome cardiologist was talking us through the process:

NATALIE (SMELLING THE DOCTOR)
Are you wearing Acqua di Giò?

DOCTOR
Why, yes I am.

NATALIE
It smells really good on you.

When we were walking through the funeral home picking out a casket for our dad:

NATALIE (TO THE FUNERAL DIRECTOR)
It would really be helpful if we could see him IN some of these before we make our choice.

Natalie always knew how to toss in a zinger just when someone was crying too hard or things got too tense, as they often did then. It was truly a testament to her strength and resilience. Natalie really had the hardest time of all of us.

She was living with our parents when they split and was only nineteen, a freshman in college, when he died.

So here we all were, the whole Rannells family, minus one very important player, walking around the Heafey-Hoffmann-Dworak-Cutler Funeral Home trying to plan Ron's final party. Some decisions were easy. He would want "On Eagle's Wings" sung at his service. He would want fried chicken at the luncheon. (Cardiologists be damned!) Other choices were harder, but they needed to be made, and quickly. We decided that we would keep Ron's last look in the casket more business casual than formal and dressed him in khakis and a polo. He wore a suit nearly every day for work. He would be more comfortable this way. We also decided that the casket should be closed. There was nothing wrong with his face when he died; he was just a more private person. We figured he wouldn't want people gawking at him in these last moments. We let our mom pick out the readings for the service and the picture for the prayer cards, and we all just sort of filled in the rest.

Because my parents were practicing Catholics, we also had a viewing and a rosary the night before the funeral. This usually happens at the funeral home, but the funeral director suggested that we hold the viewing in the church because "Ron would bring out a big crowd." I'm embarrassed to say that I was happy to hear that. I guess I had spent too much time in the theater, and the importance of a sold-out house was already seared into my brain. Not that funeral attendance numbers are recorded anywhere, but I liked that people liked my father. He was an easygoing guy, always quick with a smile or a laugh, and was popular at our school and church.

After my grandma died and I realized how much I had

let my family relationships slide, I had made a greater effort to stay in touch. Between the distance and my parents' separation, I had realized that it was up to me to cultivate some kind of relationship with my dad. Between the two of us I would generally be the one who called him to check in once a week. The conversations were brief at first, but as time went on, we got better at communicating on the phone. We really started to nail it when I was on tour with *Pokémon Live!* I would regale him with tales of disastrous performances or drunken little people getting into bar fights with locals. I loved making him laugh. It was a nice surprise. He loved those stories.

A few months before he died, he was asked to be an extra in a movie that was filming in town, native Omahan Alexander Payne's *About Schmidt.* The scene was a funeral for the wife of Jack Nicholson's character and my father played one of the mourners. He was very excited about being in this movie, not so much about being on screen, but about being on set and seeing how it all worked. Ron loved movies. He passed that on to me when I was a kid. It was one of the few activities we did together, perhaps because it didn't involve talking.

I remember speaking with him right after he filmed his scene in *About Schmidt.* I didn't know he had been a part of it. He let me go on and on about the ridiculous drama of *Pokémon Live!* and the pitfalls of performing at the Indianapolis State Fair Coliseum. When I finally got around to asking him how his week was, he casually said, "Oh, well . . . My week was fine. I filmed a scene with Jack Nicholson in Alexander Payne's new movie."

Well played, Ron. Well played.

My family felt that some of us should speak at the rosary the night before the funeral. My sister Becky stepped up to welcome everyone because she was the oldest, and I was volunteered to close out the evening because, I guess because I was the actor in the family. Becky's speech was appropriately heartfelt and emotional. Other folks got up to share stories and condolences. Natalie and I sat next to each other and quietly judged everyone's speech based on genuine emotion and quality of content.

It came time for me to share my thoughts on Ron. These are the moments when being a performer is both helpful and a hindrance. I was comfortable speaking in front of a crowd, even under these circumstances, but I was also hyperaware of what I looked like and how I would be received. I'm pretty sure I was the only man with highlights in that church and definitely the only one who was so concerned about the fit of his suit. I wanted to be heartfelt like Becky, I wanted to share good memories and say how much I loved Ron and would miss him, but as I started to speak, I realized that didn't seem right. Our relationship was complicated. In many ways, we were just getting to know each other when he died. My feelings for him were new and precious and they weren't for public consumption. Or maybe I didn't know how to articulate them yet. So instead, like any cheap actor might do, I played for laughs. I told the *About Schmidt* story and it killed. It killed so hard that a couple people started to applaud, like we were at some open mic night. I was pleased but also embarrassed that I had played it up so hard. (But I also figured Ron wouldn't have minded.)

The next day, back at the funeral home, we had a small visitation before the actual funeral began. (I didn't realize at the time how much casket moving was involved in this operation. Poor Ron was really getting shuttled around a lot.) There we sat, just our immediate family, looking at our dad, my mother's husband, lying in a casket. He looked pretty good. The makeup was subtle. He looked relaxed. As corpses go, he looked like a happy one. And yet I was still glad we didn't have an open casket. Even in the best of circumstances, something always looks a little off. I was happy to see him one last time, but also happy not to share that version of him with anyone else.

As mourners started to arrive, Natalie and I realized that the casket lid was still up. We started looking for someone from the funeral home to close it, but we couldn't find anyone. I decided *Fuck it, it's a lid. I'll just do it.* I was about to shut it when the funeral director came running in. "Don't!" he shouted. "It'll smash his face!" It turns out caskets aren't just boxes, they're complicated little machines. The funeral director had to do a whole host of things involving cranks and handles, finally lowering my dad into the box so that the lid could be shut and locked. (Locking it seemed a little excessive, but he was the professional.)

The most moving part of the day was seeing all the people who came to pay their respects. It was a real-life version of *This Is Your Life: The Ron Rannells Edition.* Coworkers, classmates, old babysitters of ours, old girlfriends of his. And the stories they would quickly tell us, the memories they would share, they were overwhelming and incredibly emotional for all of us, but I was so grateful to hear every detail. Until Suzy showed up.

Suzy was the wife of my father's high school friend Bill. I hadn't seen her in years, and I don't think my mother had, either. She arrived looking a little disheveled and clearly distraught. There was something about her demeanor the moment she walked into the room that told me, *Oh fuck. She has taken ALL the pills today.* She had on two walking casts, one on each foot, and had two canes, one in each hand. Both casts were sloppily wrapped in black trash bags, as if to protect them from the rain. It was sunny out that day, so unless she was worried about lawn sprinklers, I'm not sure what she was protecting them from. Her hair was askew, as was her makeup, and she spoke in a loud and very slurred way. She sounded like Eileen Heckart as Mrs. Daigle in *The Bad Seed*. (For those of you who got that reference, thank you and you're welcome.) She hobbled up to my mother and aggressively hugged her. She began shouting, "I loved Ronny so much! I just loved Ronny!" The she lunged for the casket. "Why is this closed?! Please let me see Ronny one more time!" No one really knew what to do. Her husband certainly wasn't doing anything to stop her. My brother Dan and I stepped in to help her. She was now attempting to pry the lid of the casket open while shouting, "I just want to see Ronny!" Thank God that funeral director had locked it. Now I saw why.

We moved her to a seat, and it was then that she *really* started to cry. "I just loved your father so much. I loved that Ronny so much." All of a sudden she stopped. She stared at me for a long time. Then she shouted, "That's not your real hair color, is it? Why would you do that to yourself?!" The scene was now complete. I started laughing and had to walk away. Pretty much everyone was laughing at this point, maybe because they all wanted to ask me the same question.

With that, Bill finally decided Suzy had done enough and escorted her out of the funeral home.

The rest of the funeral was beautiful. It all went as planned and was appropriately reverential and respectful. I only cried twice and only for a brief moment each time. The first time was when the choir sang "On Eagle's Wings," because in our church that was the ultimate funeral song. It made me realize exactly where we were in that moment—in this case, my father's funeral. And the second time was when they played taps before lowering the casket into the ground. Our dad would have liked that. He was very proud of his time in the army.

The good face I had been trying to put on started to crack. I suddenly felt like I had to take care of everyone else and comfort them while they mourned my father. People I didn't know well were coming fully unhinged while speaking to me about my dad. I was taking care of them, but I wanted to be taken care of. Natalie, Dan, and I made a silent agreement through a series of private eye rolls and looks toward the exits, and then we snuck back to our mom's house while the funeral luncheon was still going on. We had all had enough for the day. We had some drinks and sat silently with one another. It was a long process and we were glad it was over.

But it wasn't really over. Over the next week, there were a hundred little details to handle: moving all of Ron's things out of his apartment, closing his business, closing out his utilities. It was unique explaining to the cable company that, no, Ron wasn't moving, Ron was dead. Please disconnect his HBO forever. It became my full-time job to dismantle my dad's life.

I also realized that while I hadn't been away from home

that long, it had been long enough that I no longer had a place there. I didn't have friends, I didn't have a bedroom, I didn't have a car. I felt like a houseguest in a house that felt only vaguely familiar to me. I had been so focused on creating my own life in New York that it hadn't occurred to me that my family's lives were all continuing without me. Any gap I may have created when I'd left had been slowly filled in. My siblings and my mother had to start going about their normal lives again—jobs, kids, general life stuff. Their grieving wasn't over, but it was time to start trying to move forward.

After a few weeks at home, it was time for me to go back to New York. I needed to figure out what was next for me. I felt bad, like I was letting them down somehow. But they were all supportive of me getting back to my version of normal.

My seat on the flight to New York was in the last row of the plane. I didn't have anyone sitting next to me, which felt like a real win. As the plane ascended, something cracked inside of me. I felt so terrible for leaving. For leaving my mother, leaving my sisters, especially Natalie, who was so young and in such a vulnerable place in life, straddling the line between childhood and adulthood. For leaving my brother, who was in the middle of planning his wedding, which must have been so difficult in that moment. I felt guilty and selfish, and the worst part was that I felt *relieved*. I was flying away from a lot of sadness and pain, and I was flying back to a place that was all mine. I cried on that plane, while no one was watching, while no one could hear over the sound of the plane's engines. By the time we leveled off at ten thousand feet, I had stopped. I felt calm and drained.

The flight attendants started to make their rounds with

drinks and snacks. One male flight attendant was particularly attentive to me, giving me free champagne every time he passed by. I found myself flirting back. It was a fun game to distract myself from where I had been. As the plane was about to land in New York, he sat down next to me in one of the empty seats. "What were you doing in Omaha?" he asked.

I thought about what to say. Should I be honest? "*My dad died.*" Or maybe say, "*I was at a dental convention.*"

"I was visiting my family," I decided was easiest. I didn't need manufactured sympathy from a stranger.

"And you live in New York?"

"I do," I said, smiling.

He then handed me a bottle of champagne wrapped in a white napkin.

"My number is inside. Let's go out sometime."

He kissed my cheek, got up, and walked away. I was stunned. And pleased. And relieved that I didn't have to talk about where I had just been and what I had just done. I was headed back to my life and my grief, and my memories of Ron were my own. I didn't have to share them with anyone.

The Wisdom of Hedwig . . .
and Britney

AFTER RETURNING FROM OMAHA AND THE STRESS of my dad's funeral, I found myself happy to be in New York and excited to get my life back in order. Freshly graduated from Barnard, Zuzanna was in the midst of setting up her new non-academic life. She'd moved to a new apartment in Brooklyn and was working as a hostess on the Lower East Side and auditioning for whatever she could find. Now we were struggling actors together. Luckily, she still had loads of free time and was there to welcome me back with plenty of laughs and Pinot Grigio to ease the re-entry anxiety.

I got myself an apartment in Astoria, Queens, which at the time was the go-to neighborhood for financially challenged actors. I was feeling somewhat settled, but still a little off. My friend Jenn (of Theater Barn and *Footloose* fame) recommended an affordable therapist to me. His name was Thomas. I started going when I could, and I have to say, it helped me sort through a lot of what I was dealing with. Coming from a place where people didn't talk about their therapists as openly as their dermatologists, I had never really asked myself, *How do you feel about this?* Or *How did this affect you?* I was used to just barreling forward and hoping for the best. *I should have paid someone to listen to me years ago,* I realized.

I had some *Pokèmon Live!* money saved, but I was job-less for the foreseeable future. It was back to the ol' audition grind. I scanned *Backstage* religiously and tried to will an opportunity to magically appear. After weeks and weeks of searching, I managed to snag myself an audition for a show I loved, in a town I had always wanted to visit. The Zachary Scott Theatre Center in Austin, Texas, was doing a produc-tion of John Cameron Mitchell and Stephen Trask's *Hedwig and the Angry Inch*, a one-person monologue with a killer rock score that follows the adventures of a fiercely determined and wildly passionate young man in Germany who reluctantly be-comes a young woman in Kansas and, later, New York City. It's unique and powerful and was a huge success off-Broadway.

I had never seen the show in its original space at the Jane Street Theatre because it was sold out by the time I'd discov-ered it. Then, before I knew it, John, the original Hedwig, left the production entirely and I refused to see anyone else do it. (Also, I wasn't really sure where Jane Street was. This was during my first year in New York, and anything below 14th Street was a total mystery to me.)

I listened to the cast recording obsessively, memorizing every lyric and imagining all of the connective tissue that held the songs together. I also fell in love with John Cameron Mitchell and his voice. It sounded like a cry from his heart. There was a pain and power to it that I understood and was also envious of.

I went strutting into that audition with my special blend of overconfidence and fear of being discovered as a fraud. I decided I would sing "Born to Run" by Bruce Springsteen, my go-to audition number in those days. It was one of my favorite songs, and I liked singing it regardless of whether it was appropriate for the show. It fit my voice unexpectedly well, and I loved that it was about wanting desperately to leave where you are from. In this case, I figured it was appropriate-ish.

I arrived to find that, much like my first *Rent* audition, there were several men there in various stages of drag. Once again, it hadn't occurred to me that this was an option. But this time I oddly didn't care. I liked that I was one of the only guys without eyeliner. *I'll stand out,* I thought. My name was finally called and I walked into the room to find just an accompanist and the director, Dave Steakley. I sang "Born to Run," and the director watched me the whole time, never once looking at my résumé. That's always a good sign. Then Dave asked, "Do you know anything from *Hedwig*? 'Wig in a Box' maybe?"

I knew the entire score—I thought—by heart. I nodded and the accompanist began to play the song. It's an emotionally and vocally climactic moment for Hedwig, and it comes at a critical moment in the show when Hedwig is deciding to really embrace who and where she is. It started out okay, but you know how sometimes you think you know the words to a song, and then one day you are in a car with a friend and that song comes on the radio and your words don't match their words? Because your words are WRONG? That's what was happening here. I was singing in gibberish, and it occurred to me, WHILE SINGING, that in fact, I did not know the entire score. Dave was patient and let me fumble my way through a verse and a chorus. Not a total disaster, but not a slam dunk, either. He asked me to look at one of

Hedwig's speeches outside while the next person auditioned. I sat in the hallway looking at this speech and realized how much I didn't know about this show. I thought my contextual skills were pretty solid, but there was a lot happening on this page that I had not imagined while listening to the cast album on my daily runs around Astoria Park.

The guy who went in after me came out quickly. As he passed me in the hall, he looked at me with panic and said, "I thought this was a children's show! I just got back from a five-year cruise ship gig. I don't know what the hell this is!" *At least I knew more than that guy,* I thought. I went back in to read and made a split-second decision as I walked through the door. I said to myself, *Fuck it. Just do what feels right.* The whole message of the music is about accepting yourself and fighting against expectations and limitations forced on you by other people. Maybe I didn't know who Hedwig was after all, but this would be *my* version of Hedwig.

Apparently it went well, because I booked the job, and a month later I was down in Austin rehearsing. Having dropped out of college and never really gotten to do any serious academic acting studies, I poured myself into this production. I did research, I explored, I allowed myself to be bad at points. I tried things that ultimately didn't work but that were still helpful with finding out what landed and what didn't. It was exciting and fulfilling and Dave was the perfect director for me. We really got to discover this show on our own terms, away from the judgment of New York and past productions, past *Hedwig*s.

I loved doing this show, but the hours offstage grew to be very lonely. I hadn't had a ton of contact with anyone in my

family since I'd gotten to Texas. I think we were still unpacking a lot of feelings about Ron's death. That's what people
don't tell you about mourning, or at least what no one told
me: You feel better pretty quickly after the funeral. You are
relieved to get back to your routine. You start to forget that
there is a big piece of your heart that is gone. Sometimes you
feel the pain but forget why, and then you're like, *Oh, yeah.
My dad is dead.* Or sometimes everything is fine, and then
you are in a grocery store alone on a Tuesday morning and
you hear "Mustang Sally" from *The Commitments* soundtrack
playing over the store's speakers. Next thing you know, you
are openly weeping in the granola aisle. Emotion sneaks up
on you. And not just sadness, sometimes anger, too. Why
did my dad have to die at a kid's birthday party? Why didn't
his doctor do a more thorough checkup months before? And
why was my mother already dating? These are the questions
that came tumbling into my brain and eventually out of my
mouth one Saturday morning at a relatively quiet IHOP in
Austin, Texas.

My mom and Natalie had decided to visit and see *Hedwig*
about a month into the run. I was nervous for them to see it;
it was so different from anything they had seen me do before.
But I was also excited because I was really proud of this production. They would only be in town for the weekend, but
they were going to see the show twice, which was sweet of
them. They really liked it. Or at least they said they did, and
that's really all any actor wants to hear.

The next day we decided we would grab some breakfast
and go see an early screening of the Britney Spears/Kim Cattrall vehicle, *Crossroads*. I had been working day and night

since I'd arrived in Austin and hadn't had time to find all of the cool and "weird" stuff yet, so we ended up at a local IHOP. Not the most personality, but at least we knew what we were getting.

I don't know how it started. I really don't. The mood at the table was tense to begin with. Maybe it was the travel, maybe it was my mom seeing her son in drag, maybe it was too much IHOP coffee. All I know is before I knew it, we were *truth telling*. Somewhere in our minds, Natalie and I decided that a crowded pancake house on a Saturday morning was the perfect place and time to confront our mother about how angry we were that she had a new boyfriend. We hadn't planned this, but once one of us opened the door a crack, the other one went barreling through. It turned out that we both had more anger in us than we had expected. Our conversation got extremely heated and, at times, extremely loud. But being the good Midwesterners that we are, anytime the waitress approached the table to refill our coffee or see how we were doing, we slapped smiles on our faces and tried to mask the epic familial meltdown that was occurring over our Rooty Tooty Fresh 'N Fruity pancakes.

CHARLOTTE
You have a lot of fucking nerve speaking to me like that!

WAITRESS (APPROACHING)
More coffee?

CHARLOTTE
Well, that would be wonderful. Thank you so much! This is all so delicious!

And then:

ANDREW
You could have at least tried to show a little discretion!

WAITRESS (APPROACHING)
Are you all done?

ANDREW
Oh my gosh! I am stuffed! My eyes were bigger than my stomach, I guess!

THE WHOLE TABLE LAUGHS MANICALLY.

This argument continued as we paid the check and walked to my rental car. It continued on the drive to the movie theater. It continued in the movie theater parking lot. Finally, having had enough and noting that if we wanted to get good seats for *Crossroads*, we were going to have to get inside, my mother decided to end the argument definitively by shouting at Natalie and me, "I'm sorry your mother's a whore!"

With that she got out of the car and stormed away. Natalie and I sat in silence for a moment. Stunned. Saddened. Embarrassed. Vindicated. And then Natalie said, "Where does she think she's going to go?" We awkwardly and somewhat sadly chuckled and got out of the car. We found Charlotte on the steps of the movie theater with three tickets in hand.

"We are going to see this movie, damn it," Charlotte said.

If you haven't seen *Crossroads*—sorry, Shonda Rhimes—don't worry. Here's the gist: Britney and her two high school pals go on a road trip after their graduation, to find Britney's mother, who abandoned her shortly after birth. After zigzagging their way across the country, on a trip that includes boys and fights and a wildly unrealistic karaoke sequence, they land somewhere—I want to say Florida—to discover Brit's mother, played by Kim Cattrall, dressed as a zookeeper. (If you've seen the film, you know what I'm talking about.) Kim admits to leaving baby Britney, but she doesn't regret it. She essentially slams the door in Britney's face. This rejection opens Brit-Brit's emotional floodgates and gives her the artistic and personal strength to finish writing the epic ballad "I'm Not a Girl, Not Yet a Woman," which in the film starts as a poem Britney wrote. Maybe that's the most unrealistic detail in *Crossroads:* Britney is a poet.

The movie ended. We sat, in the near empty movie theater, in silence for a minute. I didn't want to move. I didn't want to have to re-enter the reality we had created at breakfast. The reality where all our cards, the genuine and the petty, were on the table. Charlotte finally broke the silence. "Well, at least I'm not as bad as Britney's mom." We couldn't help but laugh. I can't speak for Natalie, but I immediately felt selfish and regretted many of the things I had just said. My mother was not the villain here. She was a victim of loss and shitty timing and she was in pain, too. We all made our way back to the car. We didn't need to talk anymore. We had said enough for one day.

As I was getting ready for my performance that night, I couldn't stop thinking about our day, our argument. I was applying the final layer of glitter to my makeup. My insane Hedwig wig was tightly pinned to my head, my lashes were firmly glued to my eyes, my lips were aggressively painted over my own. Underneath all of that drag and in some way because of it, I could see my mother in my face. I had always been told that I looked like her, and even though I had never seen my mom in grotesque punk drag, I imagined that this was what she would look like. I recognized her in my mirror and I recognized her in my feelings, too—the loss, the anger, the sadness, the confusion that followed Ron's death.

Getting to pretend you are a different person for a living has its benefits. You literally get to walk in someone else's shoes. You get to try on a life that is very different from your own and see how it feels. See what they feel. The role of Hedwig is an absolute gift to any actor who gets to play the part. There's a lot to mine in her story, and if you are feeling angry or sad and judged or lonely, there is a place for all of that in *Hedwig*. All of the sadness about my dad went into that show. It also brought up unexpected feelings as well. Feelings about my moving to New York from Omaha. Feelings about my first sexual experience with the forty-year-old. And more recent feelings about my mother that I hadn't really allowed myself to process.

That night I lost myself on stage thinking about my mom and her life. (As I learned from *O, The Oprah Magazine*, I was having an "aha moment.") She had lived the majority of her life as a mother. She had always told us that it was all she ever wanted to do. She thought of it as her dream, her vocation. But here she was, thirty-three years later. Her children were all grown. She needed another dream. She was figuring out what would be next, just like I was doing. And my mother's new relationship and my father's death were two separate issues. One didn't cause the other, but each complicated the other. Something gently cracked inside me that

night on stage while I was singing "Wicked Little Town." I
sang the lyrics:

> *The fates are vicious and they're cruel.*
> *You learn too late, you used two wishes like a fool.*
> *And then you're someone you are not, and Junction City*
> *   ain't the spot.*
> *Remember Mrs. Lot and when she turned around.*

I loved my mom very much, and she was also in pain and
needed my love and support. In return, I knew I would receive it back from her. It was going to be a process and maybe
a constant negotiation, but it had to start from a place of for-
giveness and understanding. Just as John Cameron Mitchell
and Stephen Trask had shed some light on this moment, I
also saw that Britney Spears had helped, too:

> *I'm not a girl, not yet a woman.*
> *All I need is time, a moment that is mine.*
> *While I'm in between.*

Okay, I'm lying. The lyrics of "I'm Not a Girl, Not Yet a
Woman" were not helpful or directly healing in this moment.
But I can't think of Hedwig and that argument without also
thinking of Britney and *Crossroads*. Memories, like feelings
and Christmas tinsel, are complicated, and most of the time
they come out in a clump that needs to be pulled apart slowly
in order to make it pretty. Charlotte and I were trying. That
was the important part.

Everything Is Rosie

IF YOU ARE GOING TO ENTER INTO A CAREER IN THE arts, it's important to know that the most common feeling you will feel, and I'm talking on a daily basis, is rejection. Even if you aren't actively rejected that day, the feeling of lacking something, of losing out, is always just stuck on you. You can't shake it off, so you learn to plow ahead. You distract yourself and you build yourself up with positive thoughts and a good therapist. Trips to the gym become like a job, household errands become an all-day event. You make yourself busy while you are waiting for your career to begin.

I was born into a demographic that is given a lot of opportunity. There is no shortage of jobs for tall white guys in musical theater. There is also no shortage of tall white guys trying to make it in musical theater, but at least there were plenty of possibilities over the years. I am glad that our industry is finally starting to add some long-overdue diversity to extend those possibilities to everyone. Still, jobs are scarce. It's a hard business, but over time you toughen up. It's just a survival mechanism. You go through a few heartbreaks, and then you realize that maybe it's better to just expect less and be surprised if it actually goes your way. The problem with this method is that it numbs you. The losses and the wins start to bleed together in your mind. You stop feeling anything because everything seems so fragile. You seem so fragile. *I* was fragile.

I started learning this lesson while still in Omaha auditioning for community theater. There was a production of Thornton Wilder's *The Skin of Our Teeth*. I auditioned for the role of the Telegraph Boy.

I was too tall.

Then there was *Marvin's Room*. I auditioned for the role of emotionally disturbed teenager Hank.

I didn't seem disturbed enough.

Once in New York, as we have discussed, I had my countless attempts at *Rent*.

All the hand-knitted, striped scarves in the world were not going to make me look like I was squatting in the East Village.

And then there was the off-Broadway production of *The Fantasticks*. A job I was certain was mine.

Too tall again!

And then there are the worst rejections of all—the ones that go beyond not looking or sounding the part; the ones where you know, without anyone telling you, that you simply weren't good enough.

While I know now that these rejections helped me develop a thick skin, there is one audition story that I look back on that still stings. Not because it would have changed my life or because the show was a huge success, but because it came out of nowhere and it came during a time when I swore I was done with show business. I had told myself that I was finished with auditions and callbacks and rejection—but I got pulled back in so easily. I was completely seduced by the possibility of this long-shot dream becoming my reality.

I had come back from Austin and my production of *Hedwig* thinking that I had some momentum behind me. I was crushed to learn that no one in New York cared about a successful regional production of anything—not even one that was a personal triumph for me. I was licking my wounds and feeling generally sorry for myself when I got a phone call from one of the producers of *Pokémon Live!* His name was Norman and he ran a large production company called 4Kids Entertainment. He asked me to meet him at his office. Since *Pokémon Live!* had ended, I had periodically done voice-overs for some of their animated Saturday-morning shows. I was not booking a ton of theater work and I was happy to do it. I met with Norman, and he explained that his company had acquired a large block of time on Saturday mornings to program and they found themselves with a lot of new content but not a lot of staff. He was offering me a job to direct the voice-over part of these new animated series.

I was flattered and confused by this offer. I asked him if there would be flexibility with the schedule to accommodate my potential Broadway career. I still wanted to be free to audition if asked. Norman looked at me with a mix of sternness and sympathy and said, "Andrew, how much longer are you going to chase that? This is a great opportunity, it's more money than you have ever made, and it will put you in control of your life. I'm giving you a great opportunity here." I thought about what my dad would think of this chance I was being offered. I thought about all the rejection I had experienced in the past years. I thought about the dreams I'd had for years, and then in an instant, I changed them. I accepted the job, and days later I was working at 4Kids Entertainment.

Months passed and I was able to almost forget about the Broadway dreams. I loved going to the theater, and some of my closest friends were still acting and having successful careers on Broadway. It was painful to be so close to it but also so far away. But I was comforted by something else—stability. I had never experienced that in my adult life and it felt wonderful. Wonderful and dull, at times, but mostly wonderful. I was feeling nearly settled in this new corporate life of mine when, one day, I got an unexpected phone call from a casting assistant at Bernie Telsey Casting named Craig Burns. He had remembered me from my countless *Rent* auditions. He told me that there was a new Broadway show that Rosie O'Donnell was producing about the life of Boy George. It was called *Taboo*. There was one part still available, the role of Marilyn, an aggressive, gender-fluid party boy from the 1980s Leigh Bowery London club scene. Craig thought I should come in for the part. I was hesitant. I had banished all thoughts of returning to acting. I was living a different life now. But I was also a sucker for "signs" and "second chances," so I agreed to come in. There was a lot of music to learn and a lot of scenes, but I immediately liked the material. The part reminded me of *Hedwig* in a lot of ways. I was intrigued.

The day of my audition, I told my boss I had a doctor's appointment. I didn't want anyone to know what I was up to. I didn't even tell my friends. I went to Bernie Telsey's office with an air of "Who gives a fuck?" about me. I had a job, a real job that paid real well, and I wasn't even sure I wanted to be an actor anymore. *This will just be for fun,* I told myself. And that's exactly what I did, I had fun in that room. I had all of the audition material memorized, so I was free to do whatever I wanted physically. I rolled around on the floor. I humped the wall. I threw my water bottle at one point. I was just living my full and honest life as Marilyn, all while singing and speaking in a very broad English accent. (I had prepared by watching hours of *Absolutely Fabulous*. I just basically slurred a lot to hide any regional inaccuracies.) Craig looked stunned, or terrified, I couldn't quite tell. He said, "Can you excuse me for a minute?" He left me alone in the audition room with the accompanist. I was confused and feared he was calling the Bellevue psych ward. *Maybe I shouldn't have thrown that water bottle.*

Craig re-entered the room with Bernie Telsey, a man I had never actually seen in person. It was kind of like seeing Charlie from *Charlie's Angels*.

"Do that again," Craig said.

"Do what?" I asked.

"All of it." he said.

So once again I rolled on the floor and humped the wall. I definitely threw that bottle again, even harder this time. When it was all over, Bernie looked at me and smiled.

"We are going to bring you in to meet the director for a work session."

What the what? Director? Work session? (Honestly, I didn't know what a "work session" entailed, but now didn't seem like a good time to ask. As it turns out, it's when you work on the material with the director. I probably should have been able to figure that out.) We scheduled the work session for the following week, and they sent me home with more material and said that I should watch some films by the director Mike Leigh for my accent. (I guess *Absolutely Fabulous* was not the best choice.)

I worked and worked on that material. I got excited again about acting. I told my boss that I had another doctor's appointment and headed out for my work session. The director was a British man named Christopher Renshaw, and I quickly learned that he didn't want a performance, he wanted to see how I took direction, how malleable I was. It was fun. He was fun. I didn't feel stressed or scared, I felt at ease with him. I got the sense that he liked me. He was laughing and kind and I thought, *I think this is happening for me this time.*

Dear reader, please take note of this feeling. It's the "This is my moment" high that has shown up every time I've auditioned for something. You may have noticed that it has come up a few times in my stories. This is a feeling that plagues actors at every turn. Now, if you tank an audition, you're generally walking out of the room, thinking, *God, that was embarrassing. Better luck next time, me!* But if you get even the *slightest* glimmer of hope from someone in that room—a laugh, a smile—all of a sudden you are already mentally spending your future paychecks at Crate & Barrel. As I was packing up my things to leave, Christopher Renshaw said, "Andrew, we would like to bring you back to meet Rosie. Sound good?"

Rosie.

As in, the renowned comedian and famed talk show host Rosie O'Donnell. Rosie O'Donnell, the sole producer of this show. According to the papers, she alone was fronting the $10 million to mount this production. She had the final word. This was it. My final callback.

"Just do everything exactly as we just did it and you will be fine. Better than fine," Christopher said. *Holy shit, this is happening.* (That damn feeling again.)

Weeks went by and I heard nothing from Bernie Telsey's office. I checked in with them periodically, and their response was always the same, "You are definitely coming back. We are just having a hard time with Rosie's schedule. We aren't sure when she will be back from her Miami house." As an avid watcher of *The Rosie O'Donnell Show*, I knew all about this Miami house. She was probably barbecuing with Gloria Estefan at that very moment, while I was sweating the fate of my professional future.

Finally, three weeks after my work session, they called. Rosie was in town and it was time to come back in. "Just do exactly what you did last time," they repeated. The problem was, I didn't really remember exactly what I had done last time. I thought I did. But did I? Another problem to solve was, how was I supposed to miss another day of work unnoticed? I couldn't say I had another doctor's appointment, and I couldn't just call in sick. I needed to up the stakes. I needed to create a foolproof way to generate understanding and support. I needed something personal. I could say I had a bad breakup and I needed to take some time.

No. That seemed too weak.

I could say that I needed to escort a friend to have an abortion. I did that once when I worked at the Gap and it totally worked.

No, I got it.

I would tell my boss that I had to get a colonoscopy. It would create sympathy and give me the entire day off, and he wouldn't want to know any details. It was perfect. I went into my boss's office and explained, with slightly tear-filled eyes, that I had to have this procedure done. He was definitely sympathetic. Too sympathetic. Or maybe I had too many tears in my eyes. He hugged me and told me it was all going to be okay. I immediately felt terrible. In that moment I realized I just should have said "root canal." It was too late.

But I got my day off!

The day of my Rosie meeting, I was terrified. What if I couldn't do it? What if I couldn't replicate something I had done once a month ago? I wore the same outfit, figuring that was a good start. I got to the office, and Bernie Telsey himself greeted me. He immediately put me at ease. "You are going to be great," he said. The waiting room was empty except for one other person. Bernie noticed me notice this person.

"Andrew, this is Jeffrey Carlson. Jeffrey, Andrew Rannells. You'll both be reading today."

What fresh hell is this? I wasn't told about this. I was led to believe that I and I alone would be meeting Ms. O'Donnell today. Who the fuck is Jeffrey Carlson and why is he crashing my meeting?

Jeffrey had floppy blond hair and was wearing tight pants and a pair of high heels. I was wearing jeans, a white tank top, and work boots. I had a chilly flashback to my *Rent* audition. *Why has the idea of auditioning in drag always eluded me?!* I thought. (Quick Audition Tip: I always figure that an actor's skills should be enough, so I've never been a fan of auditioning in a full homemade costume. But more often than not, directors and casting directors don't have the best imaginations. Sometimes a homemade costume pays off. Unless it's for *Cats*. Or *Les Miz*. Or *Starlight Express*.)

"Andrew, you are going to go first." Bernie said.

That's right. I am going to go first. I am going to go book this job first, and Jeffrey Carlson and his pumps can get back on the bus to wherever the hell he came from. (I later found out he came from Juilliard.)

I was angry, and as cheesy as it sounds, I thought I would use that anger for my audition. I would funnel it into my performance just like that girl at the end of *Center Stage.* She put all of her passion into the DANCE!

I marched into the room. There she was, Rosie O'Donnell. She did not look like the Rosie on TV. There was not a pant-suit in sight. Not a single wide-collared silk top. Instead she was wearing a stretched out T-shirt, half of her head was shaved, and she was severely sunburned. But her voice sounded exactly the same.

"Thank you for coming in today, Andrew. Everyone says you are wonderful. Thank you for being so patient." She was so nice. So kind.

Okay. Just do it.

I did all of the material better than I had ever done it. All my crawling, all my throwing, all my humping—everything felt grounded, justified. I was getting laughs, the room applauded at one point. I did my final scene, which was sort of emotional, and I nailed it. I looked at Christopher Renshaw and he smiled and nodded at me. I looked at Bernie Telsey and he did the same. *I did it. I did exactly what I was supposed to do.*

Rosie applauded me.

"You are very talented, honey. Where are you from?"

"Omaha, Nebraska," I said.

"Well, you are very talented. But I am afraid this is not going to be your job."

The room fell totally silent. There was a ringing in my ears. The room seemed to blur for a moment. *What did she say?*

"You're just too masculine for this part. You should be the boyfriend. Bernie, why didn't he come in for the boyfriend?"

Bernie looked stunned. "It was already cast."

"Well, he could have done it. But I guess not now. I'm sorry, honey. You're just not right for this one."

Do not cry. Do not cry.

"Thank you for having me in," I choked out. "It was nice to meet you all."

And that was it. I was done. More than two months of auditioning for a show that I didn't even ask to audition for and it was all over in an instant. Part of me was happy that Rosie crushed that dream so quickly. But part of me wanted a couple more hours of hope. Even if they had called in two hours to say that Jeffrey Carlson booked the role, which he did, at least I would have had two more hours of thinking that my dream could come true. I got out on the street and threw all my audition materials into a trash can on the corner.

I was right to leave this horrible business, I thought. *I don't want to be in this lame ass show anyway. Fuck that. Fuck them.*

I was learning a new coping skill, one that hadn't really crossed my mind in the past. Usually I was just sad after not getting a job; I had never been this angry before. Anger felt better, more active than sadness. I decided I would curse that show. *That show is going to be a flop anyway,* I told myself. I repeated that often, in fact. If anyone mentioned the show in my presence, I would say things like, "I hear it's trash," or "Have you seen the poster? It looks like garbage!" I didn't tell many of my friends about my auditions because I was afraid I'd look like a fool for getting my hopes up. I'm sure it struck them as odd that I had such strong feelings about a show I had never seen.

In reality, the show was indeed a flop and closed quickly, which felt good, vindicating, at first. But that feeling was short-lived and didn't make me happy. It made me sad. Sad for the people in the show, sad for me for holding on to that anger for so long. It didn't serve me. I realized it was better to be sad first because it leads more quickly to happiness. Anger leads to bitterness and then sadness and just delays getting to the happy part. *Better to skip the anger next time. If there is a next time.*

I went back to the safety of my animation job and once again vowed not to be pulled into the allure of show business. I thought about all the times I had been burned. Years of disappointments and feeling not good enough. Yes, there were some minor successes along the way, but the odds seemed stacked against me. It was time to retire that dream. I would stay in my corporate life and reinvent my future. It was safer there.

Ivy League by Association

As I was resigning myself to a career in children's cartoons, Zuzanna was adjusting to life as a struggling actor. She was now experiencing all the things I had started going through years before. The survival jobs, the frequently disappointing auditions, and the occasional win that kept your spirits up were all a part of her life now. But because she was not pursuing musical theater, her options were even more limited. Non-union auditions for plays were few and far between. She was keeping herself busy, but she knew that she wanted more. And to get it, she realized that she might have to go to graduate school. She was accepted into a handful of prestigious acting programs, and while I secretly hoped that she would choose Juilliard or NYU—anywhere in the city, really—she decided on A.R.T. at Harvard. Very fancy. I was proud of her, but I was also devastated that she would be leaving me for two whole years. I remember one night in her apartment, helping her pack before she left for Cambridge. I tried to comfort myself by saying, "These two years are going to fly by. Before we know it, we will be back in this apartment unpacking these same boxes!" I didn't really believe it, but I wanted to.

Zuzanna left in July and was thrown headfirst into acting

grad school, rarely coming up for air. Weeks went by and we barely spoke. I knew she was getting settled and that she needed space to enjoy this new adventure, but I was also jealous of what she might be experiencing: new friends, artistic fulfillment, maybe romance, all without me to witness it or discuss it over magnums of white wine. Early in September, she called me and we finally had a proper catch-up. As I'd suspected, she was having a great time. There was a flurry of names that I didn't recognize and inside jokes that I didn't understand. I was happy for her but sad at the thought that my best friend was having this life-changing experience without me.

But then, a miracle. She suggested that I come for a visit. I could stay with her and meet all of her new grad school acting pals and see how wonderful Cambridge was. I loved the idea. I could use a break from the city, and the Harvard campus sounded adorable. I just assumed everything would look like *Good Will Hunting*. I asked our friend Jill, who had gone to Barnard with Zuzanna, to join me. Jill was and still is a constant source of joy and support in my life. We share an obsession with Stephen Sondheim, an admiration for the love affair of Elizabeth Taylor and Richard Burton, and a deep love of whipping up a hot appetizer for a cocktail party. As we drove to Cambridge, Jill and I confessed to each other that we were a little suspicious of Zuzanna's new academic acting friends. We were going to enter this situation with our arms fully crossed and let *them* come to *us*.

We arrived, and when we saw Zuzanna, it was as if no time had passed between us and her. I was relieved. She had become my family, and I needed our relationship to stay intact. That first night, the three of us just got drunk in Zuzanna's apartment and caught up. Jill and I talked about job woes and boyfriend troubles, and Zuzanna filled us in on her grad school romances, who she liked and didn't like, classes she was taking and acting techniques she was learning. It all sounded exciting and foreign to me, and once again I started to regret passing up a full acting school experience. I had never taken a movement class or learned how to speak properly. I'd always relied on my instincts or a good director's notes. *Did I make a mistake dropping out of college and never going back?* I wondered. *Maybe I was missing an opportunity, an experience that would be helpful to me professionally and personally. Maybe I wasn't where I needed to be.*

The following night there was going to be a big party with all of Zuzanna's classmates. While Jill and I had our plan, we also wanted to do our friend proud. And on a more honest note, we were both desperate to be liked by everyone. So that next night, we came out to play. Meaning: We got day-drunk while Zuzanna was at class and then arrived to pick her up, fully lit and ready to be the life of the party. We both really overcompensated. Even though we had planned to be pleasantly distant, we ran into the crowd basically screaming, "LOVE US!" I can't speak for Jill, but I was intimidated by these grad school actors. They seemed confident and smart. They spoke a secret language of Meisner and "tremoring" and Russian acting professors that was insufferable but made me insecure. I had abandoned my professional ambitions, and these people were chasing theirs full speed ahead. So Jill and I did what seemed most sensible: We bought everyone drinks and tried to figure out who we could have sex with.

Jill and I were a hit with Zuzanna's new friends but mostly by default. These people did nothing but go to class for twelve hours a day and had only been spending time with one another. They needed new blood, and Jill and I were happy to open our veins. Jill locked it down with a guy pretty quickly, but I was coming up empty. Most of these guys were straight and WAY too serious about acting for my taste. I can play along for a little bit, but at a certain point, I can't talk about Uta Hagen anymore.

Zuzanna swore that there was someone coming who I would love, but he hadn't arrived yet. I was getting impatient. I was just about to cut my losses and head back to Zuzanna's apartment for the night when suddenly the doors of the bar opened and in walked . . . Kaolin. Kaolin was, and is to this day, gorgeous. He is tall and handsome and has a face that looks like it belongs on a Roman coin. When he smiles at you, it feels like you've been smacked in the chest in the best possible way. When I saw him walk in, in my head, I heard that song "Kiss Me" by Sixpence None the Richer. Maybe I had just watched too much *Dawson's Creek*, but I was having a real moment. Zuzanna saw me see him.

"He's beautiful, right?" she said. "He just modeled for Abercrombie this summer. Like, he's in the catalog."

This new information was almost too much for me. Did I have the skills to make this happen? The buckets of Pinot Grigio I had been drinking led me to believe, yes. Yes, I will land this plane! (Or for you Annette Bening fans, "I will sell this house today!") I moved in. Kaolin was clearly out of my league, but he was also trapped in a grad school sexual waste-land and I was a new body who, just by existing, was appealing. Within fifteen minutes it was clear how this night would end. I think most gay men, and some women, reading this will understand what I am talking about, but for those of you who don't, let me try to explain: Sometimes with the right vibe and the right lighting and the right amount of alcohol, two people in newly fallen lust make an unsaid contract with each other through eye contact alone. There's a Sexual ESP that occurs where you lock eyes and know, "I will be seeing you shortly for sex, sir." That's what happened with Kaolin that night. We just knew.

What I didn't know that next morning, when I woke up in his bed, was that we would both start feeling, well, feelings. Feelings that felt *real*. It must have been the confluence of intense attraction and the power of fantasy that only two actors could manifest. There was an instant intimacy between us that was equal parts incredible and incredibly confusing. I needed time to investigate, but the weekend was over. It was Sunday, and Jill and I both needed to be back at work in the city on Monday. Like me, Jill had a job that was slightly soul-crushing but necessary for survival. I talked to Zuzanna about these new feelings for Kaolin. We weighed my options, and she agreed that I needed more time. "Just call in sick to work," she said.

This is a totally realistic suggestion and one that would normally work for just about any professional person. I could have just left a message for my boss that afternoon saying that I wasn't feeling well and that I wouldn't be in the next day. Simple as that. But, as you will recall, I had already used all my fake doctor's appointments plus a fake colonoscopy, so I definitely could not fall back on anything medical. It was going to have to be something complex. Something that couldn't be easily challenged. So bizarre that my boss would never even *think* of questioning it. I concocted a tale so strange that my boss was floored and, honestly, probably scared for me. I called him and told him that my friend Jill (I used her real name) had gone missing in Cambridge. I told him that she had gone home with someone she met in a bar and never returned. I explained that Jill (again, HER REAL NAME) had done this before, and while I was certain that she would ultimately be fine, I couldn't possibly leave Cambridge without her. He, of course, was sympathetic about the possible abduction of my friend and said that missing work on Monday was not a problem. As I type this, I am still baffled as to how I got away with these things. I'll bet my boss just thought I was deeply troubled and let these incidents slide.

In any event, I bought myself an extra day with Kaolin and, more important, with Zuzanna. During that day I caught a small glimpse of what it might be like to date Kaolin while he was living in Cambridge. Weekends out of New York City, Amtrak rides, collegiate-looking blazers, driving his SUV around campus, picking him and Zuzanna up after class. It all sounded romantic and fun. I could date a sweet Abercrombie model and be with my best friend almost every weekend. I decided I was in. I locked down a relationship with Kaolin in forty-eight hours, and we agreed that we would take turns visiting each other every other weekend. In reality, I was the one who did most of the traveling, because of his school schedule and because it allowed me to see Zuzanna. It was perfect for a while. It was autumn in Cambridge and it was all sweaters and changing leaves and Pump-kin Spice Lattes. And on a subconscious level, I was "playing grad school student." Much like I had "played Broadway" with Jim, the singlet-wearing chorus member in *Footloose*, I was once again hoping that some of their experience might rub off on me. If I couldn't be in grad school, I could at least date someone who was. I know that is a cockamamie line of reasoning, but that's where I was, folks. That's where I was.

After a couple months, reality set in. The commute to Cambridge was wearing on me, and Kaolin's school schedule didn't allow for much contact. Our romance was one meant for summer camps or the *Titanic*. It burned hot and bright, but only for a moment. I think those relationships are im-portant. You learn, quickly, a lot about yourself and what it is you are looking for, what is actually important. And let's be honest, Jack and Rose wouldn't have lasted on land. He was a common criminal and she was a spoiled brat. If she re-ally loved him, she would have scooched over more on that headboard.

So Kaolin and I ended. We ended with minimally hurt feelings and a clear understanding that this was really more a matter of reality and logistics. But I was still disproportion-ately sad about the demise of this brief love affair. I came to realize that it was because I wasn't going to be seeing Zu-zanna as much now. Traipsing up there every other weekend for your best friend seemed needy. For a boyfriend it seemed normal. I had created a reason, a very handsome reason, to be in Zuzanna's Cambridge world.

While she was still the same girl I loved, and the physical distance hadn't changed that, I was well aware that her life was making just a little more sense without me in it. I was jealous of her new friends, I was jealous of her new life, and I was jealous that she was following her dreams and going after what she wanted. She hadn't been happy with the opportunities she was being presented with so she flipped the script. Why couldn't I do that?

Going back to school didn't seem like a viable option for some reason. I never felt like I belonged in school, even acting school. My path would have to be different. But staying in Saturday Morning Cartoonland didn't feel right, either. Could I still do what I came to New York to do? Was it too late for me to get the thing that I wanted? I needed to make some changes.

The Tallest Man I Ever Loved

IF THIS POINT IN MY LIFE HAD BEEN A MOVIE, I would have given myself a fast-cut makeover, like Julia Roberts in *Pretty Woman* or Goldie Hawn in *Death Becomes Her*. Then, I would have bolstered my confidence like Christina Applegate in *Don't Tell Mom the Babysitter's Dead* by putting my hair in a low ponytail, smoking a cigarette, and plowing ahead. But much to my horror, this was not a movie. So I did what most adult New Yorkers do—I asked my therapist for help.

I was still seeing Thomas, and at this point in our sessions he introduced the concept of visualization. He believed that if you really wanted to manifest something in your life, you could do it by focusing all your energy and thoughts on that thing. I had been doing my own version of this all my life, so I took to it easily. I figured that this was a perfect time to restart my life, so we went through the three major areas that I could control: my career, my living space, and my love life. We made lists of all the things I wanted. In a job, I wanted something stable, something artistically fulfilling, something lucrative, and something I could be proud of. My apartment was meant to be a beautiful haven from the stresses of the outside world. And my relationship . . . well, that's where I got *really* specific. I wanted him to be:

- Taller than me
- Dark-haired
- Fit, kind, and funny (but not too funny because that was my job)
- Social, but not have that many friends (I didn't want to compete for attention)
- Creative

A list only a twenty-two-year-old could make. Please note that I started with the physical attributes.

The professional stuff was hard to control, so I quickly moved on to the living space list. I couldn't move, so I decided to redecorate. I got most of my ideas from episodes of *Trading Spaces* on TLC. They made it seem possible to change your whole world with some cans of paint and a glue gun. While I wasn't quite as ambitious as the designers on the show—I mean, I wasn't about to hot-glue hay all over my walls or nail the furniture to the ceiling like Hildi—I was feeling creative. I thought I would start with my bedroom, so I bought some new sheets. They were purple. I don't know why I thought that was a good idea. I was on my way to the Laundromat to wash those purple sheets and take control of my new and self-possessed life when I saw him. It was Todd, aka my Danny Zuko, from the Westchester Broadway production of *Grease*. He looked even more beautiful than I remembered. He was literally tall, dark, and handsome, and except for the whole being straight thing, he was exactly what I wanted.

As we started to chat, I attempted to hold my purple sheets in the most inconspicuous way possible, while sweating profusely in the June sun. Todd said he had just moved in next door to my building. I tried not to swallow my tongue at this news. Not only would I be seeing him casually all the time, I was going to need to always be on guard, have fresh breath, and be ready for a street chat. *I should probably go shopping for new walking-about outfits,* I thought. Todd said he had heard about my dad and felt terrible about not reaching out sooner. In trying to comfort him about not comforting me, I actually said the words "Oh, it's okay!" about my own dead father. I was really nailing this interaction.

Todd asked me what I was doing that night, and if I was free, would I want to have dinner with him? "It would be great to catch up," he said. Are you kidding me? Catch up? I will catch anything you want to throw at me, Todd. We made a plan to get together that night, and then I practically floated to the Laundromat.

I knew this wasn't a date, but I was still very excited.

We'd picked a spot in our neighborhood, which was mostly made up of Greek restaurants, and decided to order gyros and some beers. I didn't drink beer, but it seemed appropriate for my non-date date with this straight guy. We mostly talked about my dad and my family and the funeral and how quickly it all happened. I really opened up to him in a way that surprised me. Maybe because it wasn't a date. Then I asked Todd what he had been up to since I last saw him. He got a serious look on his face. "It's been a crazy couple of months. After my divorce I really had to think about what had gone wrong with my marriage and why." I'm going to be honest here, I zoned out for most of Todd's speech and was mainly just watching his sexy lips move and how his pecs jumped when he gestured with his hands. But I instantly became laser-focused when he said these words: "I realized that I'm gay and I wasn't being honest with myself. So . . . I wanted to tell you that, Andrew. I'm gay."

You know those moments when all time stands still? I imagine like when you drive your car off a cliff or when you see your baby for the first time? That's what this felt like. It was equal parts terrifying and also incredibly exciting. *He's gay. He's gay.* I kept repeating it in my head. I finally managed to say something supportive and vague about being honored that he chose to tell me this, and also how brave I thought he was for being honest with himself. And then we moved on. I knew from my own coming out that saying the words could be difficult, and it didn't necessarily mean you wanted to talk it all out in that moment. I followed Todd's lead and the subject was changed. The rest of the dinner was mostly professional chitchat about auditions and jobs and things we wanted to do with the rest of our summer. We walked home to our apartments, hugged awkwardly for a few seconds too long, and then I went inside in a daze of anxiety and lust.

I paced around my apartment like a tiger in a cage, re-playing the conversation over and over again, wondering if I should have said something different, if I should have acted different. Somewhere in my spiral I came to the con-clusion that maybe we had been on a date. Maybe that was his attempt at asking me out and I blew it. Thinking about this now, I have no idea how I came to this conclusion. I think it had a lot to do with my new manifesting mentality. I had a high level of self-centeredness, which convinced me that his coming out was somehow about me, but also a low self-esteem, which prevented me from believing that someone that attractive would ever be interested in me. (I blame my mother for this phenomenon that has plagued me my whole life: High Self-Worth/Low Self-Esteem. If anyone was ever making fun of me at school, she would say, "They are just jealous of you." But if I said something negative about someone else, she would say, "You aren't any better than that person. Don't say that." So which was it, Charlotte? Was everyone jealous of me or was I no better than anyone else? I digress . . .)

It struck me like a lightning bolt that the only possible action at that moment was to go back to Todd's apartment and simply ask him, "Was this a date?" And that's exactly what I did. I rang his buzzer, announced that it was me, and he let me into the building. I went to his door, where he was standing there without his shirt on, and in a more panicked tone than I had wanted, I asked, "Were we just on a date?"

Todd smiled at me. "Get in here," he said.

I did as I was told and we proceeded to have the greatest sex I had ever had in my entire life. Everything about him was perfect: his mouth, his eyes, his body. I was twenty-two years old and I was instantly in love with him. That night, I fell asleep and woke up in his arms. It was the first time I had slept the whole night through since my dad died. Everything about Todd made me feel safe. And I think I made him feel safe. He was just out of the closet and here he had a man, albeit a young man, who was mad for him and would do anything for him. It must have felt like dating a puppy.

That night began what I considered to be my first adult relationship. There was not a day in the next few years that I wasn't either with him or thinking about him. We had sex

every day we were together, often twice a day. I had never
been so attracted to anyone in my life. The intensity of this
attraction also brought about an insecurity and mania in me
that destroyed us several times. I was both Sid and Nancy in
our relationship in the way I needed him and hated him for it.

Todd, for the most part, was a real trouper. He was patient, he was understanding, he was sensitive. However, his
one major flaw was his habit of occasionally having sex with
someone else. Each time this happened, I would have sex
with someone else to get back at him, we would both cry
and promise to be better, and then we would fuck ourselves
back in love. It wasn't mentally healthy, but it was exciting.
And what did I know about relationships at twenty-two? All
I had ever been told about long-term relationships was that
they were "a lot of work." And we were definitely working.
Mostly too hard.

It's important to note that shortly after Todd and I started
dating, we were both given auditions for the new Broadway
production of *Hairspray*. The whole show was cast, but at the
last minute, they needed a new men's chorus member. He
would be one of "The Nicest Kids in Town" and understudy
Link Larkin and Corny Collins. Todd and I were not the
same type physically or vocally, and there was a twelve-year
age difference between us, so it came as quite a shock that
we would both be considered for the same role. Even though
I loved Todd, I was out for blood the day of that audition.
I got in that room and the dreaded "this is going to happen for me" feeling came rearing its ugly head once again.
Everything they asked me to do just clicked in my body. I'm
sure Todd was having a similar experience, because we both

got down to the final four. We left the audition that day in silence and rode back to Queens together, both imagining our new Broadway careers.

About two hours later we both got phone calls telling us that neither of us had booked *Hairspray*. Todd was disappointed but took it in stride. I, on the other hand, was devastated. I was truly convinced that I belonged in that show. I was cheesy, I was white, and I could Pony my ass off. The inevitable crash after the high of possibility landed hard on my heart once again. If I couldn't land this job, then what business did I have being in this business? I decided to focus on my work at 4Kids. I really thought I was done with showbiz this time.

I had a steady boyfriend and a steady job. Todd and I created a comfortable routine together, and I didn't miss being rejected by the career I wanted most. When you let yourself settle into a life that is comfortable, it's crazy how time passes. The first year went by quickly. Mondays turned into Fridays and I found myself living for my weekends. Todd and I were going to farmers' markets and flea markets, basically any kind of market, just to pass the time. There were weekend trips upstate and home repair projects. I learned how to decoupage. (*Trading Spaces* still had a big influence on me.)

Todd and I were good together—mostly. The first time we broke up, for approximately a month, was in a terribly dramatic fashion. We went on a cruise with another gay couple, friends of ours. I hated the experience. The cruise ship made me depressed. The people, the overeating, the sunburns—it all seemed so forced. No one was really having a good time, but they were all working their asses off to show that they were. We were docked in Cancún, and Todd and I got into a terrible argument in our room. I don't remember many of the details of this particular fight, but I do remember it started because he "made me feel stupid" for ordering Riesling at dinner the night before. (At twenty-three, everything is very high stakes, folks.) This argument spiraled, as they often do, into a larger conversation about me feeling controlled by Todd and Todd feeling like I ignored him when we were out with friends. The doors to the balcony were open, and the whole time we were fighting, we could hear mariachis playing various covers of pop songs. Our relationship ended during "La Bamba." Todd shouted at me, "I don't want to do this anymore!" just as the final note was played. (I'm sure he was thrilled at his accidental musical timing.) This was only midway through the cruise, so we still had three more ports to get through before we could go home. We barely spoke to each other.

This breakup was relatively short-lived. Before long we were back into our routine of weekend crafts and constant blow jobs. This was the first truly serious relationship either of us had been in. I mean no disrespect to Todd's marriage, but this was the first time his sexual preferences lined up with the person he was committed to. I understand now that being insanely attractive and having just come out of the closet, he wanted to make up for lost time. He had just discovered some new tricks and he wanted to show them off—with other people. I totally get it. I didn't at the time, but now I do. And there was a part of me that didn't fight him too hard on these periodic requests. I was madly in love with Todd, but I was also curious. We were mostly monogamous, with a handful of *Friends*-style breaks during which we would each take some exploratory sexual walkabouts.

Time passed, and a new restlessness set in after my twenty-fifth birthday. I was mostly recovered from my failed *Taboo* experience, but there was a nagging feeling deep in my soul. It was like a phone that kept ringing and ringing and I was refusing to answer it. That ringing was becoming more frequent and kept getting louder.

I remember I was directing a recording session for my voice-over job, with an actress in her forties trying to sound like a little boy in his tweens. She was screaming the lines about some nonsense, and I just realized, *I can't do this anymore.* I went into the bathroom after the session was over and I looked in the mirror. I looked sad. I looked older than I should have looked. I thought about why I had moved to New York in the first place, what I had wanted to do with my life. I thought about my dad, I thought about Grandma Josephine, I thought about the people I did community theater with in Omaha. I thought about my first acting teacher, Pam Carter. I thought about my mom and my siblings, all living their lives far away. I thought about my friends here in New York who were all chasing their dreams. I thought about Todd and how he wanted me to be happy. I thought about me at nineteen, excited to be in New York and ready for anything. I was not living the life I wanted. I had let myself down. It just clicked in my head. I was ready to answer that call.

I walked into Norman's office and I told him that I was quitting. He was flustered but he didn't fight me. I went home and told Todd that night what I had done. He was shocked and weirdly angry that I hadn't discussed it with him, and then finally, he was supportive. My first months of unemployment were exciting. I decided that I needed to move out of Queens. I needed a change, so I found an apartment in Hell's Kitchen. The whole building was filled with Broadway actors, including my friends Jenn Gambatese and Gavin Creel, and was located right by Times Square, in the heart of the Broadway theater district. It was a tiny studio, but I redecorated it to look just like Carrie's apartment in *Sex and the City*. (I was Carrie, damn it. I know, I know, everyone thinks they are Carrie.)

The excitement of change quickly became terrifying as I realized that, with the exception of my *Taboo* debacle, I hadn't auditioned in years, and now I was trying to jump back in where I had left off. There were new casting directors, new assistants, new people who didn't know me at all. I was starting all over again . . . again. I reached out to a few people I still knew in various casting offices and told them that I wanted to start auditioning. To my relief, a few remembered me, most importantly Rachel Hoffman and Craig Burns. Rachel got me an audition for an off-off-off-Broadway production of a spoof musical of the film *The Karate Kid* called *It's Karate, Kid! The Musical*. (The wording and punctuation of the title were to avoid paying legal fees. It was a classy operation.) I was cast as the villain, Johnny Lawrence, and while there was basically no money involved, I was so happy to be acting again. It was a terrible production filled with talented people and I was having a blast. I remember Todd coming to opening night and being slightly horrified by the show's content but ultimately happy to see me doing what I loved.

In the middle of this short run of *It's Karate, Kid! The Musical*, Craig Burns called me with an audition. For *Hairspray* on Broadway. It was the exact role I had auditioned for years earlier, and it was available once again. But as much as I was enjoying acting again, and had recommitted myself to my career, I just couldn't do it. There was too much pressure, too much pain surrounding that show. Because I'd had friends involved in that production, including my friend Jenn, I'd seen it multiple times over the years. I'd attended their opening-night party, their Tony Award party. I'd always managed to put on a happy face and be there to support my friends, but it was painful to be reminded of that rejection. With *Taboo*, the show opened and closed and it was almost as if it had never happened. With *Hairspray* . . . it just kept lingering. It wasn't going anywhere. It was my John Waters–shaped White Whale. Taunting me. Laughing at me. I decided I wouldn't go to the audition.

That night, after my off-off-off-Broadway performance, my friend Kevin Cahoon and I went out for a drink, and I told him about the call from Craig and the replacement audition the following day. "I'm not going," I told him. "It's too much." Kevin, who is normally very mild-mannered, became very stern with me. "Andrew, you have to go. This is what you wanted and now it's being presented to you once again. You have to go."

I hadn't thought about my manifesting powers in a long time. I had given up believing that there were signs from the universe or energy that one could manipulate through sheer will, but I heard Kevin's words and they hit me square in the heart. He was right. I was asking for an opportunity and I was being given that opportunity. It would be wasteful and disrespectful to myself if I didn't take the chance.

The next day I went to the audition. I didn't tell Todd I was going, for two reasons: He hadn't been called in and I didn't want to upset him. Also, I didn't want to be embarrassed when I didn't get it again. This wasn't about a job, this was about me confronting what had scared me off years ago. There weren't many guys at the audition. I wasn't nervous, I wasn't scared, I just did it. I just did the material the way I wanted to do it. I felt strangely calm, not quite confident, but calm.

When I left that audition—and I'm hesitant to use this word—I felt a peace come over me. Not the "This is my moment" feeling that had usually plagued me, but peace. I had faced the show that had broken my heart and I was still standing. I was going to perform in *It's Karate, Kid! The Musical* that night, and I felt like I was almost exactly where I had wanted to be. I got back to my apartment, and as I was entering the building, my phone rang. It was Craig Burns. "Andrew . . . you got it. You are going to be in the chorus of *Hairspray* on Broadway." I got it. I got it. I was going to play "Fender" (the tallest of The Nicest Kids in Town). That was one of the happiest moments of my life, standing in the dusty entryway of my apartment, still sweaty from the audition and hearing those words.

Todd was already inside my apartment, waiting to have dinner before my show. I told him the news. He was quiet for a moment. His face tightened in a way that I couldn't quite read. Was it emotion? Pride? Indifference? Then he said, "You beat me."

"What?" I asked.

"You beat me," he repeated, and not warmly. "You got there first."

I felt like he had punched me in the stomach. He was the first person I'd told, and that was his response. He pivoted quickly and hugged me and congratulated me, but the words had already been said. I hadn't known we were competing. But apparently we were.

I called my mom, I called Zuzanna. They were both so sweet and thrilled, albeit surprised, by the news. My *Karate Kid* castmates were all happy for me, at least to my face, and we celebrated that night. Todd even came out to meet us and joined in the celebration. I put his words out of my head. *Karate Kid* closed a few days later, and I still had two weeks before rehearsals for *Hairspray* started. They happened to be the two weeks over Christmas and New Year's, and Todd came to Omaha with me. I am certain my family talked nonstop about *Hairspray* and how excited they were for me. Todd was mostly quiet about all the *Hairspray* business. He was sweet to my family, but he was mostly quiet.

When we got back to the city, my good friend Sean Dooley invited us to a New Year's Eve party at Christina Ricci's apartment. Sean had gone to high school with her and they were still close. I had only met her a few times, but she was incredibly sweet and very funny and I was excited to get this New Year's invite. Todd was not as excited to go, but I insisted and he finally conceded. The party was everything one would expect from a young Hollywood star. There was tons of booze, tons of food, and famous musicians and actors everywhere. I was levitating, I was so excited to be there.

This is living! This is what I wanted New York to be, and now seven years after moving here, I finally found it! When strangers would ask me what I did, I proudly announced, "I'm in *Hairspray* on Broadway." I mean, it wasn't exactly true yet, but it would be soon. I could tell Todd was having a miserable time. He was barely speaking to anyone and hardly making eye contact with me.

We kissed tentatively at midnight, and he asked almost immediately if we could go home. I didn't want to. I wanted to stay and celebrate this night and what felt like a new chapter in my life. But we left. We rode home in the cab in silence. We got ready for bed in silence. We lay next to each other in silence. We didn't have sex that night. We didn't really touch, either. I was angry with him, and I wanted him to be happier for me than he was. I wanted him to understand what this meant to me. Broadway. Finally. I fell asleep formulating the conversation I would have with him in the morning about how hurt I was. But I was optimistic that we could move forward. This was something that just had to be addressed. I knew it could all be sorted out.

When I woke up on New Year's Day, Todd was gone. He wasn't in the bathroom, he wasn't in the kitchen, he was gone. I looked at my phone, and I had a voicemail from him from 5 a.m. that morning. I was afraid to listen to it, but I did.

"Andrew, I can't do this. You are clearly on your way to someplace else, someplace without me. And it seems like you are going there fast. I'm happy for you. But that was my dream, too. I just don't think I can stand here and watch someone else do it before me. I'm sorry. I love you."

That was the first time, and the worst time, I had my heart truly broken. Everything was supposed to be falling into place now. I had a job I loved, I had an apartment I loved, and I was with a man I loved. This is what I had been dreaming of, trying to manifest, journaling about for years. This was supposed to be my time to have it all and keep it all. I was reminded of *Tales of the City*. No one gets all three at once. It took me a while to realize that my plans were not everyone else's plans. That I couldn't, and I still can't, force everyone else onto my vision board. That's not how life works. I was certainly learning it wasn't how my life worked.

I was devastated. There were phone calls to Todd and tears and shouting and more tears. Phone calls to Zuzanna and Sean and talking and speculating and switching violently between being angry and being broken. Trying to piece together what I had done wrong. It was dark out, and I was still in the clothes I had slept in the night before. I sat on my couch, confused and lonely. But there was a voice inside me, rising. It was the voice of my very practical, very stoic, very Midwestern ancestors again. While they may not have known anything about callbacks or headshots, they knew the value of hard work and getting back up even after you were dealt a blow. I realized that ethic had been passed on to me by my parents and their parents and their parents before them. The voice said:

"You are still here in the city that you have always wanted to live in. You have created a home and a life in the wild frontier of Manhattan. You have taken many risks, and while it was never on your time frame, those risks have paid off. You left Omaha and the safety of your family, you left school, you left a job that provided you with security, and it all led you to exactly where you wanted to be. You are going to be on Broadway. You are going to be in the chorus of *Hairspray* on Broadway. You got it, Andrew. And you deserve it. Now find yourself a plot of land and a good woman and start a family, god damn it! Spread our family seed!" (Okay, I didn't hear that last part, but I imagine my rural ancestors might have been slightly confused by some of the details of my life.)

I knew I was going to be heartbroken over Todd for a long time. I also knew that I would never get back together with him again. This was too hurtful to forgive. I couldn't compromise myself and my dreams again for anyone. It was New Year's Day 2005, and it was time to take stock of what I had: I had incredible friends. I had a great place to live. And I had a job that I had always wanted. I might have been missing a few things on my list, but that was okay. That list was going to have to keep changing anyway.

"Hairspray, Wow!"

THE THING ABOUT AMBITION IS THAT WHILE YOU can imagine many of the details of your dreams with great specificity—the joy of performing, the applause, the feeling of walking through the stage door every night—there are plenty of details that you couldn't possibly imagine correctly. The tediousness of learning complicated tenor harmony lines. The twinge of suspicion and self-doubt when you find out you are miraculously the same size as the person you are replacing and can wear all of his costumes without a single alteration. The feeling of being an outsider in a group of people who have been working together for years, and never being sure when or if you will ever break into their circle.

I quickly learned that rehearsing a Broadway show alone is a lot harder than I'd thought it would be. I had never replaced anyone in a show before; I'd only started from scratch with everyone else in the cast on the first day. *Hairspray* had been running for three years at this point, and most of the people I had known in the show had moved on to other projects. And while I was friendly with the actor I was replacing, he was moving on to another Broadway show. I was on my own.

The actual act of learning the show was odd. I rehearsed with a stage manager and a choreography assistant who was a swing in the show. A "swing" is neither a crass nickname like "The Village Bicycle" nor is it a comment on one's bisexuality, it is a title. Generally speaking, swings know every role that the ensemble plays—all the choreography, all the staging, all the music and lines. Every Broadway production has them, in case anyone in the regular cast is out of the show because of sickness or a scheduled day off, and they can go on for any role at a moment's notice. It's an extremely difficult job that requires a lot of mental acrobatics to keep all of the roles straight in your head.

A man named Rusty taught me every number, every scene, in a rehearsal room located blocks away from the lights of Broadway. Since these sessions were always just the two of us, I had to try to imagine a stage full of people around me at all times, which was a real challenge, since I was already struggling to remember all of the dance moves and music. And I didn't have much time to learn it all. I would rehearse eight hours a day with Rusty for only ten days, and then I would get one final rehearsal with the entire cast on stage. A couple days later, I would be in my first show in front of a Broadway audience.

After I rehearsed all day, I would go to the theater at night and watch the show, comparing what I had learned that day to what was actually happening on stage. I had never worked that hard in my life. I was terrified about forgetting something or losing my place in the show, and anxiety was quickly overtaking excitement in my brain. I had also never been in the ensemble before. I had only played principal roles. It was immediately clear that this was going to be a totally different experience for me. There were little featured moments for everyone in the ensemble, but for the most part you were there to support the leads and blend into the background. There was a lot of humility involved.

But who am I kidding? I wasn't that humble. A large part of my job at *Hairspray* was also to be an understudy. I would cover three of the lead roles in addition to my nightly job of playing Fender. I understudied Corny Collins, the host of the *Bandstand*-like show that The Nicest Kids in Town were a part of; the utilitarian "Male Authority Figure," who played every character part from the "Hobo Flasher" in the opening number to "Mr. Spritzer," the president of the hairspray company; and most important, I understudied Link Larkin, the Frankie Avalon–like heartthrob who Tracy Turnblad, the show's irrepressibly optimistic heroine, falls in love with.

Link was the role I was most right for, and it's the one I most wanted. While learning my Fender duties, I was secretly already teaching myself the Link Larkin track. Link was also one of The Nicest Kids in Town, so most of his choreography was similar to mine, and in some cases simpler. Plus Link got two numbers, a solo in the first act and a quartette in the second. I desperately wanted to play that part; I knew I would nail it if just given the chance. I didn't know it at the time, but I was quickly turning into someone that I had only seen in movies. I was going from understudy to *HUNGER-study*. I was Eve Harrington. I was Nomi Malone. I was instantly frustrated Broadway chorus boy Andrew Rannells.

I was not alone in my hunger. Most of the other members of the ensemble covered lead roles and wanted them just as badly as I wanted Link. For many of us, it was our Broadway debut. For others, it was their fifth or tenth Broadway show.

Two people intimidated the hell out of me: Barbara Walsh and Jonathan Dokuchitz. Barbara was playing Velma Von Tussle, the controlling and bigoted producer of *The Corny Collins Show*, and Jonathan was playing Corny Collins. I had seen Barbara on the 1992 Tony Awards as Trina in *Falsettos*, and I had seen Jonathan on the 1993 Tony Awards as Captain Walker in *The Who's Tommy*. I couldn't believe that I was going to get to work with these people. The Tony Awards had been my window to Broadway from Nebraska, and the fact that these actors were also in my first Broadway show made this dream all the more surreal.

Before I knew it, my rehearsals were coming to an end and the night of my Broadway debut was fast approaching. Zuzanna was still in Cambridge at this time, so I knew she couldn't make it to my first night. It might seem strange, but I don't recall discussing a visit with my mom or the rest of my family for my opening in *Hairspray*. At this point I had been in New York for seven years, and I think in that time I'd had four or five visits from various family members. It was easier for me to go there to visit them. They all had lives and some had small children, and the idea of them visiting for my first night on Broadway just didn't seem practical. It didn't make me sad, exactly, it just seemed like a given. I knew they would come eventually. And I didn't have Todd, so there would be no roses from him that evening. I told myself that it was better that I wouldn't know anyone in the audience my first night. I was nervous and stressed, and I just needed to focus on getting through the show. I would give myself the gift of having this experience alone. It was my dream; I had dreamed it by myself, and I would achieve it by myself, too.

The day of my final rehearsal arrived. I put on my costume and stepped onto the stage. The cast, none of whom were in costume, sweetly applauded for me. I was starting to feel like I was a part of the group, like I truly belonged there. The rehearsal went well, too well in fact; I did everything perfectly. I didn't feel that nervous. I worked like a musical robot, hitting every mark like a sniper. At the end of the show, I was dancing the finale in a high tower far upstage with the rest of the ensemble. When the number ended, the whole cast turned upstage and applauded for me again. I looked down at that cast, my new family, and was completely overwhelmed with gratitude and joy. Having never been put into a Broadway show before, I thought I was supposed to say something, so I said, "Thank you all so much for your support and patience today. I am really honored to be joining this cast and I can't wait to be on stage with you in front of an audience. Thank you."

Apparently speeches from new cast members were neither required nor expected. I remember seeing several smiling faces, but then I also saw some looks that said, "Who the hell is this kid?" I didn't care. This was my moment. I was going to take it.

I went home to my apartment after that rehearsal, exhausted but energized. I was days away from making my Broadway debut. It was almost too good to be true. I was particularly careful crossing the streets on my way home for fear of being hit by a car. I had watched too many Movies of the Week as a kid to not think there might be some kind of cosmic retribution for getting what I wanted. I made it home safely and sat down in my little apartment. I was vibrating with excitement from the day's activity. I wanted to talk to someone, I wanted to share it. But with who? I realized the only person I wanted to call was Todd. I had leaned on him for four years. I had cried with him and celebrated with him. I needed him. But he had made it clear what his feelings were about me and *Hairspray*. He couldn't be happy for me. We hadn't spoken since New Year's Day and the silence was painful, but I knew it was necessary. I was going to have to hold myself up this time.

And then my big day finally came. That's another thing I hadn't anticipated about going into a long-running Broadway show—that my big opening night would be just another Tuesday for everyone else. A Tuesday in January no less, the Monday of months. But I was determined to make it special for myself. I arrived at the theater and found flowers from Zuzanna, my mom, and the rest of my family. They knew how important this was to me, and even if they couldn't be there in person, they certainly made their support known. I was very touched.

The cast was sweet and congratulatory, too. There are many beautiful traditions in the theater, and even if you aren't feeling your best or most excited on a Tuesday night, you still rally around someone when it's their first night and shower them with "Break a leg!" and supportive hugs. Even though I didn't know any of these people very well, they were making me feel at home.

Hairspray begins with a fantastic opening number called "Good Morning, Baltimore." Tracy Turnblad is alone on stage and the ensemble, now including me, is dancing in silhouette behind her. Then the scrim that is hiding the cast flies up, revealing all the denizens of Baltimore dancing in joyful unison. I was standing behind the scrim waiting for the moment of the big reveal. The moment when the lights of Broadway would hit my face and I could officially say, "I have made my debut and my dream has come true." I took a second to take in my surroundings. The sound of the orchestra, the feeling of the costume, the gratitude and joy I felt in my heart. I closed my eyes and thought, *Thank you. Thank you. Thank you.* I didn't know who I was thanking exactly. Everyone, I guess. The moment had come for the scrim to fly up and for me to step into that light as we all sang the chorus, "Good morning, Baltimore!" I opened my eyes and started to sing, "Gooooooood," and everything was black. I could hear the music, but it was totally black.

I've died, I thought. *I've died or I am having a stroke brought on by too much joy and gratitude. This is my moment of reckoning. This is how I go down.*

"Broadway Hopeful Dies On Stage the Second He Makes His Debut."

The actress on stage next to me, Becky Gulsvig, put her hand on my back.

"The automation is down. Don't worry. This happens sometimes. We just have to restart the show."

What?! Restart the show? This is my Broadway debut! There aren't supposed to be mechanical glitches! Everything is supposed to be perfect! The stage manager made an announcement to the audience, "Ladies and gentlemen, we apologize for the inconvenience. Due to technical difficulties, there will be a brief pause. Actors, please exit the stage."

There was a loud collective groan from the audience

followed by excited chatter. We all shuffled backstage. The cast huddled around me, laughing and hugging and assuring me that this didn't happen often. Jonathan Dokuchitz put his arm around me and said, "Happy opening night, kiddo." All of my first-night jitters, all the adrenaline, was sucked out of me. I felt an immediate crash. I felt slightly doomed and immediately panicked. *What if I can't get it back? What if I can't rally? What if I broke Broadway?* I wanted Zuzanna there. I wanted Todd there. I wanted my mom and my dad and my grandma and my whole family there. I wanted to share this moment, the beauty and the absurdity, with people I loved. *Why didn't I ask anyone to come tonight? Why did I have to try to do this by myself?* I needed support. I needed love. I should have asked for it.

The stage manager told us that the problem was fixed and that we would start exactly where we had stopped. Becky Gulsvig took me by the hand and walked me out on stage. She held my hand until the music started again. I will always be grateful to her for that kindness. *At least I have a memorable story,* I thought to myself. This time the scrim flew up as planned and we all sang, "Good morning, Baltimore!" The audience burst into applause. It was the magic of live theater. These people had enjoyed a special treat; they got to see something go wrong. I would quickly learn that audiences love that—they love to see the cracks almost more than seeing the polished product. Their applause signified that we had all made it through together, that now we were back on track. I knew it wasn't true, but I also took some of that applause to mean, "Welcome to Broadway, Andy Rannells."

I wish I could say that my first performance was perfect.

That I remembered everything and I nailed my debut. I did not. That false start really threw me off my game. My nerves got the best of me and I was a mess. In the second number, "The Nicest Kids in Town," I nearly killed Richard Blake, the actor playing Link Larkin. (I swear this was not a *Showgirls* moment. It was a real accident.) At one point in the number, all the men jump in between the women and over the open orchestra pit, landing on the lip of the stage (the technical term is the "passerelle"). It was maybe a six-foot jump from takeoff to landing. It's a thrilling moment when it happens correctly. On this night, however, the brightness of the lights and the loudness of the orchestra sent me into a tizzy and I temporarily lost all spatial awareness. I jumped in front of Richard, cutting off his path and nearly knocking him into the orchestra pit. I was so scared that I almost fell off the front of the stage and into the audience. I quickly got back on track shouting several "I'm sorry"s to Richard in the process.

Then came the Nicest Kids roll call. Every character steps forward and says his or her name. I boldly jumped into the spotlight and shouted, "Fender!" And the craziest thing happened; there were shouts from the audience. Like a cheer. For me. But from who? Who would have done that? My already tentative performance focus was compromised once again. I nearly forgot where I was supposed to stand next. Becky Gulsvig once again came to my rescue with a nod to my mark. (Thank you, Becky.)

The show went by quickly. There were no more attempts at murdering poor Richard and no more technical delays. My show wasn't flawless, but it was a start. I was just going to keep doing it night after night, and I knew that it could only get better from here. I was standing in my final spot in the high tower at the back of the stage. Again, I was taking in the cast, the set, all the color and light and joy. *Don't forget this moment,* I thought.

The crowd was on their feet and the lights from the stage bled into the audience, illuminating their faces. I looked out into the audience. *I might not have anyone in the crowd who knows how hard I had to work to get here,* I thought, *but I feel their support tonight. I feel their love even if they couldn't be here.*

But I was wrong. There in the orchestra were my childhood friend Randi, my friend Jill, and most surprisingly, Zuzanna. They were all there cheering and waving. I waved back, too surprised to cry. They had seen it. They had shared this crazy, exciting night with me after all. I couldn't believe how lucky I was to have friends like that. From that tower I could see all the way to the back of the theater. Standing behind the last row of seats, I also saw the outline of a tall man whose shape looked familiar to me. I couldn't see his face, but I knew it was Todd. I was thrilled and then angry and then sad, and then I quickly put it out of my mind. I wasn't going to let him take this moment from me.

I walked out of the stage door and there were my friends. I still couldn't believe it. "How are you here?" I asked Zuzanna.

"I took the train in from Boston this afternoon. I have to go back first thing in the morning, but I couldn't miss your Broadway debut!"

This time, tears came. I hugged my friends and was grateful they had known what I needed more than I did.

"Did you see Todd?" Randi asked.

"I did," I said. "Is he still here?"

"No," Jill said sort of sadly. "We saw him leave."

I think Zuzanna sensed my mood shift. She generously and wisely changed the subject. "Let's get a drink to celebrate!"

My Broadway debut was a little rough in some ways but beautiful in others. I knew this was the start of a new life. But this time, unlike the new beginnings in my past, I felt like I had my feet firmly planted underneath me. I had friends, real friends in this city who loved and supported me, and I loved and supported them. I'd had romantic relationships that, even if they didn't last, all taught me something valuable, from gems of emotional wisdom like "vulnerability doesn't mean weakness" to more practical lessons like "always write 'Deposit Only' on the back of your checks when endorsing them on the off chance you lose them before you make the deposit." I had maintained and even deepened my relationship with my family, especially with my mom, and I didn't allow the distance to make me feel alienated from them. It took work, and would continue to take work, but I could still have a place in their lives.

I knew that Manhattan was not a grid below 14th Street. I knew the pizza place on 45th and Ninth wasn't the best pizza in the neighborhood, but it was the nicest and stayed open the latest. I knew to never tell the cabdriver if you were going to Queens or Brooklyn *before* getting into the cab. I knew that if you needed a bathroom in Union Square, you should use the one in ABC Carpet & Home. It's nicer than the one at Barnes & Noble.

And while I'd had professional triumphs that weren't widely celebrated by the masses, they were crucial to my development as an actor. I could lose myself in a role and yet bring my own personal touch to it. I might not have a formal education in acting, but I had figured out how to do the work to get me to where I needed to go. And I knew Pokémon were NOT people. They were weird, annoying creatures that could only say their own names.

I had amassed a lot of knowledge in my years in New York so far, and while there was more to be learned, my life wasn't just starting, it was continuing. I was not at the beginning. I was well on my way.

But here is something I quickly discovered about ambition and achieving your dreams: Once you taste it, you want more. It had always been my dream to be on Broadway. I had told myself that I *just* wanted to be in a show. I didn't care what my role was, I *just* wanted to experience being on a Broadway stage. But when I got the chance to live this dream, it didn't take long for me to dream a bigger dream. (Thank you, Maya Angelou by way of Oprah Winfrey.)

Don't get me wrong, I was extremely grateful for my chance to play Fender, but I couldn't help but imagine what it might feel like to be Link. And who knows what would be possible after Link? Were more shows possible? Other roles? Other opportunities? This pattern of dream swapping would both drive me insane and be key to my success in the future. But that was all to come later.

As I walked back to my apartment after my first night on Broadway, I remembered my first night living in the city. A cab drove past me, and I thought maybe there was a scared kid inside, a kid who was new to the city, who was over-whelmed. Maybe he or she saw me walking home with confi-dence and pep and assumed that I had always lived here, that I'd always fit in. I hope that kid saw me and thought, *I want to be that guy. I want to belong here.* I had done what I had come to do. I was excited for whatever was next, whatever that might be. I felt proud of what I had accomplished. I was happy. I was actually happy. I had become one of the people on the street who knew where he was going.

Acknowledgments

As you have learned, my first professional theater job was a production of *On Golden Pond* at the Firehouse Dinner Theater in Omaha, Nebraska. I was fourteen years old. A remarkable woman named Louise Filbert was playing Ethel (the Katharine Hepburn role), and she taught me a valuable lesson. On opening night of that production she said to me, "Just like there is an opening night, there will be a closing night, so try to enjoy every second in between." I have always tried to remember that. While I'm not always great at actually *doing* that, I have never had an opening night since then where I didn't think of Louise's words.

In reflecting about those early days in New York, I was pleased to see that most of the names that kept coming up were people I am still extremely close to to this day. My best friend, Zuzanna Szadkowski, is still my best friend. I am still incredibly close with Jill Madeo, Sean Dooley, Gavin Creel, and Jenn Gambatese. All of the exes I mention in this book, I am still on good terms with. (If I didn't mention you, we are not.) There are names that are not mentioned in this book that played a pivotal role in making it all happen: Rachel Glickman, Nikki M. James, Patti Murin, Cameron Adams, Christie Smith, Blair Kohan, Matthew Inman, and Bill

Clegg. Without Bill Clegg I wouldn't have had this opportunity. He believed in me and he fully tricked me into writing this book. And I will always be grateful to him for that.

Most important, my family is still my family. Rebecca Britt, Julie Rannells, Dan Rannells, and Natalie Whitney. Siblings are a weird thing, sharing little pieces of yourself— your sense of humor, your face—with the people you land in this world with. In my case, I feel like I won the sibling lottery. They are not only some of the coolest and funniest people I know, I also legitimately like them as humans. As adults, we all have very different lives, but we are bonded together in our love for one another, our dark sense of humor, and our love of beef and pork products. A special thanks to my sister Natalie, for reading these pages and telling me when I had gone too far or not far enough.

Finally, there's my mother, Charlotte. By far the most loving human being I have ever encountered and ever will. She has claimed that she has had nothing to do with any professional success that I may have achieved. She says that I was born with ambition and she's unsure of its origin, and that she simply stayed out of my way and things just happened as they did. In writing these stories, in remembering the past, I can say with one hundred percent certainty, she is wrong.

She gave me confidence when I lacked it, humility when I needed it, and love when I didn't deserve it. She pushed me in quiet ways, and sometimes loud ones, to be who I wanted and needed to be. She bought me a Malibu Barbie when I asked for one as a five-year-old, and encouraged me to take acting classes at nine when I was struggling to figure out what my place was. She came to every show and she never told me I was good when I wasn't. She was honest and caring and strong, and she showed me how to be a good person, and that you can always be polite without being a pushover. Thank you for giving birth to me, Charlotte, and thank you for taking your job as a parent so seriously and so lovingly. And, Charlotte, after reading these pages, if you read anything that you have questions about or anything that is unclear, especially any sex stuff, just ask Natalie to explain it. (You're welcome, Natalie.)

About the Author

ANDREW RANNELLS is an actor, singer, and performer best known for originating the role of Elder Price in *The Book of Mormon* and playing Elijah Krantz in HBO's *Girls*. A Tony and Drama Desk nominee and Grammy winner, he has also played Hedwig in *Hedwig and the Angry Inch*, King George III in *Hamilton*, Whizzer in *Falsettos*, and, most recently, Larry in *The Boys in the Band*. On the small screen, he has also appeared in *Black Monday*, *The Romanoffs*, *The New Normal*, and *The Knick*. Rannells's film credits include *A Simple Favor*, *Why Him?*, *The Intern*, and *Bachelorette*. His writing has been published in the *New York Times* "Modern Love" column. This is his first book.